the series on school reform

Ann Lieberman, *Senior Scholar, Stanford University*   Joseph P. M̶c̶ ̶, New York University

SERIES E̶

(Continued)

the series on school reform, *continued*

MATHEMATICS PROFESSIONAL DEVELOPMENT

IMPROVING TEACHING USING THE PROBLEM-SOLVING CYCLE AND LEADERSHIP PREPARATION MODELS

Hilda Borko
Jennifer Jacobs
Karen Koellner
Lyn E. Swackhamer

Forewords by
Jennie Whitcomb
Paul Cobb

TEACHERS COLLEGE PRESS
TEACHERS COLLEGE | COLUMBIA UNIVERSITY
NEW YORK AND LONDON

NATIONAL COUNCIL OF
TEACHERS OF MATHEMATICS
1906 ASSOCIATION DRIVE | RESTON, VA 20191-1502
www.nctm.org

Published simultaneously by Teachers College Press, 1234 Amsterdam Avenue, New York, NY 10027, and by NCTM, 1906 Association Drive, Reston, VA 20191-1502

The research projects featured in this book were funded by NSF Award No. 0115609 through the Interagency Educational Research Initiative, and NSF Award No. 0732212. The views shared in the book are those of the authors and do not necessarily represent those of the NSF.

Chapter 3 contains an adaptation of "Disc-Ness" (math problem) from the Balanced Assessments Tasks, created by Judah L. Schwartz and Joan M. Kenney in cooperation with members of the Balanced Assessment Group at the Harvard Graduate School of Education. This material is based upon work supported under National Science Foundation Grants MDR-9252902 and ESI-9736403 (subcontracts from the University of California, Berkeley and Michigan State University), and with supplemental funding from the American Academy of Arts and Sciences, the Boston Public Schools, the Cambridge Public Schools, and the Noyce Foundation.

Chapter 5 contains an adaptation of "Painted Cubes" (math problem) from *Fostering Algebraic Thinking: A Guide for Teachers Grades 6–10* by Mark Driscoll, 1999, Portsmouth, NH: Heinemann. Copyright © 1999 by Education Development Center Inc. Reprinted by permission of the publisher. All rights reserved.

Chapter 7 contains an adaptation of "The Gas Tank" (math problem) from *Best Buys, Ratios, and Rates: Addition and Subtraction of Fractions*, by Bill Jacob and Catherine Twomey Fosnot, 2007, Portsmouth, NH: Heinemann. Copyright © 2007 by Catherine Twomey Fosnot. Reprinted by permission of the publisher. All rights reserved.

Library of Congress Cataloging-in-Publication Data is available at loc.gov

Borko, Hilda.
    Mathematics professional development : improving teaching using the problem-solving cycle and leadership preparation models / Hilda Borko, Jennifer Jacobs, Karen Koellner, & Lyn E. Swackhamer ; forewords by Jennie Whitcomb and Paul Cobb.
        pages cm. — (The series on school reform)
    Includes bibliographical references and index.
    ISBN 978-0-8077-5655-3 (pbk. : alk. paper) — ISBN 978-0-8077-7379-6 (ebook)
        1. Mathematics teachers—Training of. 2. Mathematics—Study and teaching—Research. I. Jacobs, Jennifer (Jennifer K.) II. Koellner, Karen. III. Swackhamer, Lyn E. IV. Title.
    QA10.5.B67 2015
    510.71—dc23   2015001826

ISBN 978-0-8077-5655-3 (paper)
ISBN 978-0-8077-7379-6 (ebook)

Printed on acid-free paper
Manufactured in the United States of America

22   21   20   19   18   17   16   15   8   7   6   5   4   3   2   1

Contents

Foreword

Jennie Whitcomb

This book speaks to teacher and school leaders and district curriculum specialists who are interested in innovative professional development (PD). In practical terms, the book introduces the Problem-Solving Cycle (PSC), a teacher-led model that fosters teachers' learning about mathematical content, student thinking, and instructional practice. Through vivid vignettes, readers see and hear the model in action. In addition, the authors provide research evidence to demonstrate the impact of the PSC on teacher learning, instructional practice, and student learning. Thus, this book provides a compact, comprehensive guide to a body of research and practice that takes teacher learning seriously. Though oriented to mathematics instruction, the book speaks to all who care about building teacher learning communities centered on both academic content and student thinking.

A fundamental premise of this book is that teacher learning is a career-long endeavor. To implement reforms in mathematics education, including the Common Core State Standards (CCSS), teachers need time both to learn the mathematics more deeply and to build their instructional repertoire. Critiques of typical PD activities, such as one-shot workshops provided by outside experts, persist because quality teacher development occurs so infrequently. More recently, the idea of professional learning communities has taken hold. Although such groups do bring teachers together to discuss a book or watch videos, they do not always live up to their potential as vibrant forums where teachers are intellectually and practically engaged. It remains safe to say that too often current professional learning opportunities do not help teachers develop new knowledge and make needed shifts in their teaching practice that will, in turn, spark student growth and achievement. This book delivers a powerful vision of the kind of ambitious and sustained teacher learning experiences that teachers, and by extension their students, need.

The PSC model involves a cycle of three workshops that a teacher facilitator typically leads in his or her school building. The first workshop focuses on doing mathematics together; that is, the teachers work through a mathematical problem that they will later present to their students. The teachers generate and compare multiple solution strategies, they identify the fundamental mathematical concepts, they plan how they will adapt and teach the problem in their respective classrooms, and they anticipate where students may get stuck. Then they teach the problem with their students, and the lessons are videotaped. In the second workshop, the facilitator selects and guides a discussion of video clips of the lessons as they unfolded in the teachers' classrooms. By looking at the clips as well as artifacts of students' written solutions and explanations, the facilitator presses teachers to examine and analyze student thinking and sense-making. In the third workshop, the facilitator selects additional video clips and guides the group to discuss the teacher's role and instructional moves. The narrative and dialogue included in this book offer a ringside seat, one that brings the workshops to life so that we see the arc of teacher learning possibilities.

The PSC offers a refreshing shift because it positions teachers as workshop leaders and because it weaves together several innovative approaches to teacher learning. First, the PSC gives teachers time to play with and explore their academic content. Second, through the use of video, it presses teachers to take risks and make their practice public. Third, it directs teachers' deep attention to their students' thinking. Indeed, noticing students' thinking may be the most important facet of the PSC. When teachers really hear students' reasoning and meaning-making, they both build new knowledge of mathematics for teaching and find inspiration to try new approaches in their instruction that better serve each learner.

The PSC model emerged out of two multiyear research projects. This volume presents a cogent, hands-on introduction that helpfully illustrates for district and teacher leaders in accessible, clear detail how teachers engage in workshops and how to develop the human capital needed to implement this model at scale. Teachers deserve well-designed opportunities to continue learning across the continuum of their career, and this book affords a glimpse into a solidly researched and highly practical approach to engage teachers as learners of their content, their students' thinking, and their practice.

—Jennie Whitcomb, University of Colorado at Boulder

Foreword

Paul Cobb

With the implementation of the Common Core State Standards for Mathematics (CCSSM) and associated student assessments, schools and districts across the United States are under pressure to improve the quality of mathematics teaching. We know from research on classroom teaching and student learning that mere elaborations and extensions of current instructional practices will not suffice. Instead, most U.S. teachers will need to significantly reorganize the way that they teach mathematics if their students are to develop both conceptual understanding of core mathematical ideas and procedural fluency, as specified by the new standards. We also know from research on mathematics teaching and on teacher education that teachers' development of classroom practices aligned with the CCSSM will require sustained support for an extended period of time. School and district leaders therefore are faced with the challenge of designing and implementing such supports, which might include teacher professional development, content-focused coaching, and teacher collaborative communities.

Unfortunately, the research base on which school and district leaders can draw as they engage in the critical work of improving the quality of instruction is extremely thin. Although research on students' mathematics learning has made substantial progress over the past 25 years and research on mathematics teaching has truly come of age in the past 10 years, the problem of how to improve the quality of mathematics teaching and learning on a large scale remains underresearched. External providers are all too ready to sell a bewildering array of programs to schools and districts, with few based on solid research. In this context, it is quite an understatement to say that the work of Hilda Borko, Jennifer Jacobs, Karen Koellner, and Lyn Swackhamer in developing, investigating, and refining empirically grounded models for supporting mathematics teachers' and mathematics teacher leaders' ongoing learning is timely. The work reported in this book addresses the challenges faced by school and district leaders while also contributing to our understanding of how to support large-scale instructional improvement that is aligned with the CCSSM.

The Problem-Solving Cycle model for supporting teachers' learning that Borko and her colleagues describe is entirely consistent with current research on high-quality teacher professional development. For example, this model emphasizes the interrelations among all three aspects of the instructional triangle: central disciplinary ideas, students' developing reasoning, and teachers' classroom practices. It also highlights the importance of teachers analyzing classroom artifacts and representations of classroom practice such as classroom video recordings, mathematical tasks, and copies of student work. In addition, it indicates the value of teachers practicing and receiving feedback on specific instructional practices from both a skilled facilitator and their peers. Moreover, the model aims to support the development of school-based teacher learning communities with a common agenda for improving the quality of instruction and student learning— at least as important to the implementation of improvement initiatives as teacher buy-in.

The Mathematics Leadership Preparation (MLP) model for supporting facilitators in enacting the PSC model with groups of teachers breaks new ground. The research base on content-focused coaching and teacher leadership is extremely thin in mathematics and in other subject-matter areas. For example, research has not yet identified aspects of coaching expertise beyond being effective mathematics teachers and having relatively deep mathematical knowledge for teaching. In addition, research currently provides little guidance on the types of activities in which coaches should engage groups of teachers to support them in improving their classroom practices. The work reported in this book therefore moves the field forward and will be of interest both to school and district leaders and to researchers who are interested in designing, implementing, and investigating coaching initiatives not just in mathematics but also in other subject-matter areas.

In discussing the PSC and MLP models, Borko and her colleagues are careful to explicate the core principles of each, thereby distinguishing between their necessary and contingent aspects. This gives others who will use the models leeway to adapt the models to their own local contexts while also demarking modifications likely to be detrimental. Detailed guidance of this type is unusual and reflects the 10 years of systematic research and design work that underpinned the development of the two models.

—Paul Cobb, Vanderbilt University

Preface

We wrote this book as a resource for educators who are interested in providing ongoing, structured learning opportunities for mathematics teachers. We present two models—the Problem-Solving Cycle model for mathematics teacher professional development and the Mathematics Leadership Preparation model for the preparation of mathematics PD leaders. Both were developed and field-tested as part of two research projects conducted over the past decade and supported by the National Science Foundation (NSF). These models offer a vision and a vehicle for site-based PD facilitated by teacher leaders, focused on topics of primary interest to mathematics teachers: mathematical content, classroom instruction, and student learning. We intentionally designed the models so that they can be tailored to meet the specific needs and interests of participating teachers and administrators. We encourage readers to consider whether and how these adaptable models might be useful in their own, unique circumstances, and in what ways they might adapt the models to ensure their effectiveness.

As a context for understanding the PSC and the MLP, it seems important to present the timeline of our research. Although our efforts at developing these models began over 10 years ago, in many ways we are still at the beginning of this journey. We recognize there is a long road ahead that involves disseminating our research findings, sharing our stories, conducting additional research, and learning from the experiences of our colleagues in the field. We hope that by writing this book we are opening a door and inviting interested others to join us on this journey.

We began envisioning and shaping the PSC in 2003 as part of a research grant to generate novel ways to support middle school teachers to teach algebra to their students. The grant was called "Supporting the Transition from Arithmetic to Algebraic Reasoning," or STAAR for short. Over the course of about 5 years, the PSC took shape as a structure for conducting teacher PD and showed clear promise for producing the desired outcomes.

At first, we imagined the Problem-Solving Cycle as a professional learning community in which teachers would dive deeply into selected mathematical problems and video from their own classrooms in order to improve their knowledge of algebra and their ability to effectively teach it. Over time, as we worked with a group of middle school mathematics teachers

across several school districts in Colorado, the PSC evolved into a more nuanced model for teacher professional development, and we identified both
components of the model that are critical to maintaining its integrity and
components that can be modified. For example, we determined that the PSC
can be readily applied to support teachers in any mathematical content area,
not just algebra. Components that are central to the integrity of the model
include teachers collaboratively solving a selected mathematical problem,
teaching that problem in their classrooms, and then examining video from
these classroom lessons. In addition, the model is designed to be iterative,
prompting teachers to engage in continuous cycles of professional learning.

One of our goals in the STAAR project was to document precisely what
the PSC model entailed so that individuals outside of our research group
could lead it. To this end, we created a PSC Facilitator's Guide, which can
be accessed at cset.stanford.edu/psc, along with other supporting materials
intended for use by individuals who are interested in carrying out the PSC
with teachers.

In 2007, we began work on a new research grant, which involved an
extensive investigation of the impact, scalability, and sustainability of the
PSC. The project was entitled "Toward a Scalable Model of Mathematics
Professional Development: A Field Study of Preparing Facilitators to
Implement the Problem-Solving Cycle," or the iPSC project. A central goal
of the iPSC project was to design, implement, and research a model to prepare and support teacher leaders to facilitate the PSC. This model, which we
call the Mathematics Leadership Preparation model, consists of an annual
Summer Leadership Academy and Leader Support Meetings throughout the
following academic year, and develops leadership skills integral to the effective facilitation of the PSC. As part of the iPSC project, we worked closely
with one large suburban school district in Colorado to prepare mathematics
teacher leaders in that district to facilitate the PSC in their middle schools. In
addition to providing information about how to support PSC teacher leaders, conducting the iPSC project helped our research team understand more
about features of the PSC that are more and less challenging for facilitators
and the potential of the model to impact teachers and students on a large
scale over time.

The descriptions and analyses of the PSC and MLP models presented in
this book are based on data from the two NSF grants discussed above—the
STAAR project and the iPSC project. In some cases, our analyses draw only
on data from the STAAR project, and in other cases they draw only on
data from the iPSC project. Throughout each chapter, as we present these
analyses we strive to make clear from which project the data are drawn,
and when we highlight data from the iPSC project we reference the relevant
project year(s).

In addition to these two projects, members of our research team have
informally used the PSC and MLP models with a few other school districts

across several states for smaller-scale projects. Although we do not present specific data or analyses from those projects, they have informed our thinking over the years.

Working on this book together provided an opportunity for us to reflect on the knowledge we have gained by designing, implementing, and researching the PSC and MLP models, and to pull together research findings from the two initiatives and several cohorts of teachers and teacher leaders. We gained new insights into the PSC and MLP as we discussed the various sets of research findings, and as we wrote and rewrote the chapters. We hope that as you read the book and share our experiences, you will also gain new insights into the value of focused, ongoing mathematics PD. We are optimistic that the PSC and MLP models have much to offer the field of mathematics education, particularly as a vehicle to support K–12 mathematics teachers as they strive to ensure the success of all their students.

Acknowledgments

There are many people whose help and support have made this book possible. During the STAAR project, we were greatly aided by Cecily Abel, Kim Bunning, Eric Eiteljorg, Jeff Frykholm, Mary Pittman, Mary Nelson, Craig Schneider, Chris Willis, and Aaron Young. The iPSC project strongly benefitted from the efforts of Cecily Abel, Erin Baldinger, Melissa Colsman, Joanie Funderburk, Helen Garnier, Adam Van Iwaarden, Tyrone John, Edit Khachatryan, Carolyn King, Charmaine Mangram, Rachael Risley, Sarah Roberts, Sara Kate Selling, Rajeev Virmani, and Ed Wiley. Colleagues too numerous to cite have helped us conceptualize our research on the PSC and MLP, but we wanted to especially thank the external evaluators and members of the Advisory Board for the iPSC project: Maria Blanton, Jodi Crandall, Damian Betebenner, Megan Franke, Dan McCaffrey, Kay McClain, Jim Middleton, Judy Mumme, Nanette Seago, Miriam Sherin, and Barry Sloane.

Several colleagues who share our commitment to improving teaching and teacher professional development provided insightful feedback on manuscript drafts: Karin Brodie, Melissa Colsman, Charmaine Mangram, Joanie Funderburk, Miriam Sherin, Katherine Sun, and Jennie Whitcomb. Marie-Ellen Larcada-Smith, senior acquisitions editor at Teachers College Press, and Ann Lieberman, series editor for the Series on School Reform, encouraged us to write the book, waited patiently until we felt we had the perspective we needed in order to reflect on and share our experiences, and then provided invaluable guidance as we drafted and redrafted the prospectus and several versions of the initial chapters. We hope that the book reflects the good advice of these generous colleagues.

We are especially grateful to all the teachers who have participated in our studies. They welcomed us into their schools and classrooms, most often with video cameras and microphones in hand, and tirelessly provided us with copious amounts of data. They are the true pioneers in this journey to explore a new model of mathematics professional development.

MATHEMATICS PROFESSIONAL DEVELOPMENT

CHAPTER 1

Introducing the Problem-Solving Cycle

The PSC gives me a professional development model to use across all the middle schools in my district. When we rolled out the Common Core State Standards here, I already had a structure in place that allowed my teachers to collaboratively learn and then analyze their teaching practice related to CCSSM practices.

—Joanie Funderburk,
secondary mathematics coordinator, Cherry Creek School District

Today, more than ever, educational leaders and administrators are seeking out professional development opportunities for teachers. They are looking for PD models that can accommodate large-scale, system-level implementation of their reform directives and promote the learning of all students. Ideally, educational leaders want PD that they are confident will result in improved teaching and increases in student learning. The demand is increasing for PD models that can be implemented by teacher leaders working in their own schools, and that are flexible enough to accommodate the latest calls for reform as well as the specific needs of a particular school. Local administrators and professional development leaders are looking for models that can support initiatives such as the Common Core State Standards for Mathematics (National Governors Association Center for Best Practices & Council of Chief State School Officers, 2010), Learning Forward's *Standards for Professional Learning* (Learning Forward, 2011), and the National Council of Teachers of Mathematics's *Principles to Actions* (NCTM, 2014), as well as trends such as using data to inform practice. Models that have been carefully articulated, researched, and used successfully with a variety of teachers across schools and districts are particularly appealing. This book introduces two such models: the Problem-Solving Cycle model to support the professional growth of teachers, and the Mathematics Leadership Preparation model to support the professional growth of teacher leaders.

The PSC is a research-based model of PD that promotes teachers' learning and teaching of mathematics in line with reform principles, and in ways that are personally relevant to individual participants. This model is structured as a professional learning community that is typically school-based and led by a teacher leader at the school. It incorporates the core features of effective PD that have been identified in numerous research studies (e.g., Desimone, 2009; Loucks-Horsley, Stiles, Mundry, Love, & Hewson, 2009). That is, it focuses on subject-matter content and instructional practices, provides opportunities for teachers to participate actively and collaboratively in a professional community, and is ongoing and sustainable over time. There are many advantages of using the PSC model, such as the fact that it is highly adaptable and is focused on specific problems of practice that are of interest to the participating teachers and administrators. Additionally, it can be tailored to highlight federal, state, district, and school-based initiatives that are ever-changing and ongoing in the life of a teacher.

At this unique historical juncture, school districts across the United States are in the midst of widespread adoption of the CCSSM. For most mathematics teachers, this means that they must teach new content, using new instructional materials, while facing increased scrutiny of their classroom practices and students' learning. The intentionally flexible nature of the PSC allows teachers to engage in conversations and experiences during their PD time that directly target areas of need, as identified by the district, school, or teachers themselves. Furthermore, because the PSC is intended as a long-term model, these areas of need can be continually revisited and modified over time. For example, a school or district might decide to focus initially on one of the Standards for Mathematical Practice described in the CCSSM on the basis of a needs assessment. That focus could then shift to a different Standard for Mathematical Practice once the group determines they are ready to move on.

WHAT IS THE PSC, AND HOW DOES IT ENHANCE TEACHER KNOWLEDGE AND PRACTICE?

When teachers engage in the PSC, they become part of a professional learning community with other teachers, typically from within their own school or district. This community engages in mathematical problem solving, examining video of classroom teaching, and sharing ideas about teaching and learning mathematics. Another central component of the PSC model is a focus on teachers' own classrooms. For example, during PSC workshops the group watches and discusses video that comes entirely from participating teachers' classrooms. Additionally, in PSC workshops teachers consider aspects of context, culture, and linguistic diversity that are directly relevant to supporting the needs of their students.

Each cycle of the PSC begins with teachers working together on a selected mathematical problem. They analyze the mathematical concepts embedded in the problem, consider how students develop an understanding of those concepts, and discuss correct and incorrect ways that students might approach the problem. The objective is for teachers to take part in discussions that will help them think about important mathematical content from different perspectives, and to generate ideas about supporting their own unique groups of students in learning that content.

After teachers have discussed a selected problem together, each teacher modifies the problem and creates a lesson plan tailored to his or her own students. The teachers then teach the lesson with the modified PSC problem to at least one of their classes, and the lessons are videotaped. Teachers bring this video footage and student work to the next two PSC workshops, and together with their colleagues, they use the video and student work as a springboard for analyzing and discussing their experiences.

The PSC facilitator plays an important role by choosing appropriate video clips from the unedited footage and guiding the discussions to focus on selected themes. The video clips and associated conversations generally highlight student thinking and/or instructional moves. For example, as teachers watch a clip, the facilitator might encourage them to consider the development of students' mathematical thinking in a particular content area, strategies to support English language learners (ELLs), or what it means to apply a specific mathematical practice standard in the given context.

By electing to participate in the PSC, teachers demonstrate their commitment to broadening their knowledge base and, consequently, to becoming better able to support their students' learning of mathematics. Taking part in the PSC affords teachers the opportunity to become part of a strong collaborative and supportive learning community. As part of this community, teachers can contribute to the selection of goals for the workshops, including personal goals they have for learning mathematical content and exploring new pedagogical practices. Most important, the PSC offers a structure for helping teachers meet these goals, providing them time to think deeply about important mathematical content, the nature of students' reasoning, and effective mathematics instruction. The opportunities for deepening knowledge and improving practice that the PSC provides are increasingly critical for teachers as they strive to meet the demands of new initiatives such as the CCSSM and teacher accountability.

Developing Mathematical Knowledge for Teaching Through the PSC

Participating in the PSC enables teachers to develop an essential type of knowledge that has been labeled "mathematical knowledge for teaching" (MKT), which refers to the professional knowledge that mathematics teachers need to effectively carry out the mathematical work of teaching. Prominent education researcher Lee Shulman (1986) argued that teachers draw on both subject-matter content knowledge and pedagogical content knowledge when they orchestrate their classroom lessons. Deborah Ball and her colleagues (Ball, Thames, & Phelps, 2008) extended Shulman's work into the field of mathematics education and coined the now commonly used term *MKT*. As shown in Figure 1.1, MKT is multifaceted and incorporates both subject-matter and pedagogical content knowledge.

The PSC and mathematical content knowledge. The content knowledge that teachers draw on includes both "common" and "specialized" knowledge of mathematics. Common content knowledge can be defined as a basic understanding of mathematical skills, procedures, and concepts acquired by any well-educated adult. Specialized knowledge refers to a deeper, more nuanced understanding of mathematical skills, procedures, and concepts that is particularly relevant to teaching and learning. Our research indicates that PSC workshops promote teachers' specialized content knowledge when they discuss multiple solution strategies for selected problems, carefully unpack student errors, consider how to provide accurate mathematical explanations, and share developmentally appropriate mathematical representations.

The PSC and pedagogical content knowledge. Deborah Ball and colleagues (2008) propose two distinct components of pedagogical content knowledge: knowledge of content and teaching, and knowledge of content and students. In the language of MKT, both components are essential to teaching. When making instructional decisions and reflecting on their teaching, mathematics teachers draw on a sophisticated understanding of which instructional practices are most appropriate for teaching specific content, and how best to support their students' thinking as they learn that content.

Figure 1.1. The Mathematical Knowledge for Teaching

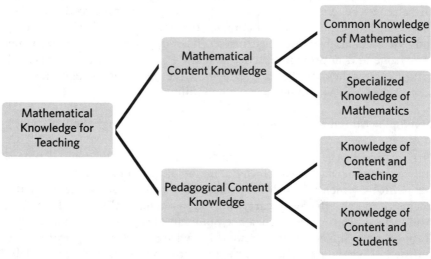

The PSC model supports the development of both components of pedagogical content knowledge by engaging teachers in focused lesson-planning activities and in critically analyzing instances of teaching and learning that occurred when they taught the PSC problem. PSC workshops promote teachers' knowledge of content and teaching when they do the following collaboratively:

- Explore the most appropriate strategies and materials for a lesson
- Modify a problem to meet the needs of their students
- Consider how to sequence content to facilitate student learning
- Examine the instructional pros and cons of different representations
- Discuss ways to improve their instructional practices the next time they teach a lesson with related mathematical content

PSC workshops foster teachers' knowledge of content and students when they engage in activities such as the following:

- Predicting how students will approach specific mathematical problems
- Anticipating student errors
- Interpreting incomplete student ideas
- Considering how to respond to the various correct and incorrect pathways that students explore

The various components of MKT are inextricably intertwined in teachers' instructional practices and are woven into each PSC workshop. In the classroom, teachers must routinely make decisions that draw on all aspects of their knowledge as they engage in the numerous, complex activities of teaching. The PSC provides a space for teachers to tap into and enhance their knowledge as they plan, implement, analyze, and reflect on specific lessons. Different knowledge strands are foregrounded in individual workshops, and in keeping with the flexible nature of the model, the needs and interests of particular groups of teachers can drive precisely which aspects of MKT are highlighted at any given time.

Improving Teaching Through the PSC

As the educational community strives to improve learning outcomes for all students, teachers are frequently asked to use instructional strategies that differ from what they experienced themselves as students. Current standards and reform efforts in mathematics education encourage teachers to plan and implement instruction that builds on students' existing knowledge and promotes the development of both skills and conceptual understanding (CCSS, 2010; NCTM, 2000). These standards encourage teachers to be aware of and use instructional moves that are sensitive to students' needs, utilize student-generated ideas, engage students in mathematical practices, and foster deep understanding of mathematical concepts.

The PSC provides a safe forum for teachers to discuss their prior teaching and learning experiences, and to generate ways to improve their instructional practices. In PSC workshops, teachers individually and collectively view, reflect on, unpack, and discuss their classroom instruction. They consider whether or not the students understood the targeted content, if there were challenges in teaching mathematical concepts and practices, or how they might have taught the lesson more effectively. Other aspects of classroom practice that teachers might discuss in PSC workshops include their experiences:

- Launching a problem
- Identifying student misunderstandings
- Asking for clarification of ambiguous explanations
- Handling student errors
- Drawing connections among mathematical representations
- Facilitating discussions that promote conceptual understanding

These types of conversations support teachers as they try to reconcile or reconstruct their teaching practices in line with new reform initiatives and meet the needs of the students in their classes.

THE PSC PROCESSES AND HOW THEY UNFOLD

Gaining Mathematical Knowledge by Collaboratively Solving Rich Problems

Rich mathematical problems are an integral component of the PSC model, laying the foundation for teachers to participate in a productive learning environment and gain valuable MKT. We are often asked what we mean by "rich mathematical problems." We define rich mathematical problems as those problems that meet the following criteria:

- Address several critical mathematical concepts and practices
- Are accessible to students with different levels of mathematical knowledge
- Contain multiple entry and exit points
- Encourage a variety of solution strategies

In each PSC cycle, teachers work with a selected problem through a series of interconnected workshops. These workshops entail solving the problem and preparing to teach it, and then analyzing the teachers' own and other group members' implementation of the problem. When teachers solve the rich PSC problem, they collaboratively explore multiple solution strategies, share ideas about the mathematical concepts and practices that are embedded in these strategies, and consider ways of adapting the problem to ensure that it is accessible to all students. In workshops subsequent to teaching their PSC lessons, teachers have opportunities to further explore the complexities of the mathematical concepts that the problem entails, and the affordances and limitations of various representations and solution strategies.

Using Video Clips and Classroom Artifacts

Another central feature of the PSC model is the use of video recordings of participating teachers' own PSC lessons and, to a lesser extent, student work produced during these lessons. Video and other classroom artifacts serve to bring the teachers' classrooms into the PD setting, making them available for study, reflection, and discussion. Teachers view short video clips from one another's lessons in order to anchor conversations and highlight particular PD goals. Video can be viewed repeatedly and from different perspectives, enabling teachers to closely examine one another's instructional practices and students' mathematical thinking and learning. Although any video of classroom instruction is likely to prove meaningful for teachers, there are strong arguments for using video from participants' own classrooms as is done in the PSC. Video from teachers' own classrooms situates their exploration of mathematics teaching and learning in a more familiar, and potentially more motivating, environment than video from unknown teachers' classrooms.

Building Professional Learning Communities

Developing and maintaining a professional learning community is a hallmark of a successful PD effort. The PSC offers teachers the opportunity to actively participate in and cultivate such a community. Throughout the PSC workshops, teachers work collaboratively to develop their mathematical understandings and to explore ways of improving their teaching. Because these PSC practices have the potential to expose teachers' limitations or weaknesses, they may be uncomfortable or threatening to participants. At the same time, when teachers do begin to share their ideas and especially video recordings of their teaching with colleagues, they have the opportunity to create an atmosphere of openness and trust that is rare in other professional learning environments. For these reasons, the development and maintenance of a productive learning community around mathematical problem solving and analyzing video is an integral component of the PSC model.

PSC facilitators must explicitly attend to developing communication norms that enable challenging yet supportive discussions about teaching and learning. They must encourage teachers to maintain a balance between respecting individual community members and critically analyzing issues in their teaching. In our experience, PSC participants overwhelmingly express the positive nature of the experience, noting that the strength of their bond as a community increases over time, which allows them to pursue relevant goals more deeply. The use of video, in particular, is touted by most PSC participants as central to their professional growth. They report that both reflecting on their own footage and seeing clips of their colleagues in action help them better understand their students' thinking and learn new teaching strategies.

PSC FACILITATORS

The PSC model is designed to be implemented by a knowledgeable facilitator who plans and leads each workshop. PSC workshops can also be conducted by cofacilitators when appropriate for a particular context. Facilitators of the PSC might be mathematics teachers, department chairs, coaches, district-level leaders, or other teacher educators with leadership capabilities, a deep understanding of mathematics, and knowledge of current state, local, and school-based initiatives. Additionally, ideal facilitators are knowledgeable about the PSC model and are enthusiastic about using it to work with teachers.

In developing the PSC model, we learned a great deal about effective strategies for leading the workshops, as well as techniques for preparing and supporting facilitators. We also identified several areas in which novice PSC facilitators are likely to need support. These include engaging teachers in productive mathematical work, leading discussions about student reasoning and instructional practices, and building a strong professional community. We drew upon this knowledge to develop our Mathematics Leadership Preparation (MLP) model and other resources for PSC facilitators.

OVERVIEW OF THE BOOK

In the chapters that follow, we provide a detailed look at the PSC and MLP models. Chapters 2–5 are focused on PSC workshops and activities for supporting teacher learning. In Chapter 2 we describe and illustrate exactly what the PSC entails and share lessons learned from our experiences using the PSC. Chapter 3 presents vignettes that illustrate typical activities in each of the three PSC workshops. Chapter 4 focuses on the importance of video in the successful implementation of the PSC model, and Chapter 5 summarizes the key findings from our research regarding the impact of the PSC on teachers and students.

Chapters 6–8 take up the MLP model, which prepares teacher leaders to facilitate the PSC. In Chapter 6 we provide a detailed description of the MLP and share insights from our experiences conducting this leadership program. Vignettes in Chapter 7 illustrate typical activities in the two components of the MLP model: the Summer Leadership Academy and Leader Support Meetings. Chapter 8 summarizes key findings from our research on teacher leaders' facilitation of PSC workshops.

In the final chapter, we provide a case study of one school district that implemented the PSC and MLP. Throughout the book, we feature the voices of many PSC participants by using quotes from interviews, examples from PSC workshops and MLP meetings, and images of changing classroom instruction. At the end of the book we include a list of published journal articles and book chapters related to the PSC and MLP models, where interested readers can find more information about our research methods, data analyses, and findings.

CHAPTER 2

Specifics of the PSC Model

In this chapter, we dive more deeply into the specifics of what the PSC model entails. These specifics are derived from our research on the model and how we, as the developers, have implemented it with teachers, schools, and school districts. While it is entirely possible to "do the PSC" using a modified structure (as we will discuss further throughout the chapter), our intention is to make explicit the focus, goals, and activities that we anticipate would be incorporated in any given implementation of the PSC.

The PSC consists of a series of three interconnected PD workshops, organized around a rich mathematical problem (see Figure 2.1). Each iteration, or set of three workshops, uses a different mathematical problem and highlights designated topics related to student learning and instructional practices. The structure of the PSC enables teachers to share a common mathematical and pedagogical experience, providing a foundation upon which to build a supportive community. Video also plays an important role, serving as a springboard for reflection and discussion about mathematics teaching and learning.

At its core, the PSC provides a focus and structure to school-based professional development for mathematics teachers. Underlying these structural elements is a great deal of flexibility that is intentionally built into the model. For example, facilitators construct their own goals for every cycle of the PSC and each workshop in a cycle. They choose the mathematical content area, the mathematical problem, the video clips to view, and the pedagogical lens through which to discuss them (e.g., launching the lesson, students' mathematical misconceptions, teacher questioning). Teachers are expected to modify the selected problem and construct individual lesson plans that reflect the needs of their own students. As we discuss later in the chapter, even the original three-workshop design of the PSC can be adapted to suit the needs and practical constraints of individual groups of teachers. For example, some groups have chosen to hold four meetings each semester instead of three, using one meeting to work on the PSC problem and a separate one to plan their lessons. This degree of flexibility is critical in affording individual groups of teachers the opportunity to take ownership of the PSC and make it relevant and responsive to their circumstances.

Figure 2.1. The Problem-Solving Cycle Model of Professional Development

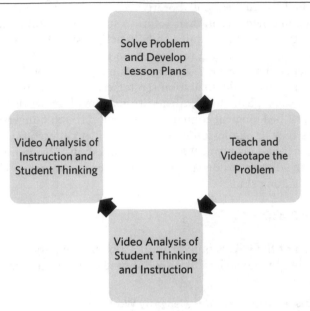

All of the workshops in the PSC model of professional development are designed to enhance teachers' knowledge of mathematics for teaching and improve their instructional practices. Different goals and knowledge strands are emphasized in each workshop through the kinds of artifacts that are selected, the activities designed around the artifacts, and the framing of those activities. As shown in Table 2.1, Workshop 1 emphasizes developing teachers' specialized knowledge of the selected mathematical content and, to a lesser extent, their pedagogical content knowledge; Workshop 2 emphasizes developing knowledge of content and students; and Workshop 3 emphasizes developing knowledge of content and teaching. However, as is true during moment-to-moment classroom teaching, participants in the PSC model inevitably tap into—and hopefully extend—all aspects of their knowledge of mathematics for teaching as they engage in the workshop activities. In the following sections, we describe the central goals, key activities, and foregrounded knowledge within each of the three workshops. Then, in Chapter 3, we share vignettes illustrating these components of the workshops in practice.

PSC WORKSHOP 1:
SOLVE THE PROBLEM AND DEVELOP LESSON PLANS

The central goal of Workshop 1 is to support the development of teachers' mathematical content knowledge, especially the specialized content knowledge that relates to the selected PSC problem. Most of the workshop time is devoted to teachers collaboratively working on the PSC problem, debriefing the mathematics in their solution strategies, and making connections among the strategies. Additionally, teachers spend a substantial portion of Workshop 1 generating unique lesson plans that will meet the needs of their students. The teachers identify learning goals, modify the problem as necessary, predict student solution strategies, and structure their lessons with specific pedagogical moves. An additional aim of the workshop is to enhance teachers' pedagogical content knowledge through conversations that take place as they design lesson plans and consider different approaches to teaching the selected problem. We call this workshop "Doing for Planning" to highlight the dual focus on supporting teachers' problem-solving and instructional planning skills.

Selecting the Problem

Each iteration of the PSC is built around a rich mathematical problem that is selected either by the facilitator or collaboratively with teachers. Teachers

Table 2.1. Goals, Activities, and Knowledge by Workshop

	Central Goals	Knowledge Emphases	Key Activities
PSC Workshop 1	Develop the content knowledge necessary to teach the PSC problem effectively in the classroom	1. Specialized content knowledge 2. Pedagogical content knowledge	1. Solve the PSC problem and debrief solution strategies 2. Plan to teach the PSC problem to their students
PSC Workshop 2	Analyze student thinking with respect to the mathematics of the PSC problem	Pedagogical content knowledge, especially knowledge of content and students	Analyze video clips or student work using guiding questions that focus on students' mathematical thinking
PSC Workshop 3	Analyze the role played by the teacher when implementing the PSC problem in the classroom	Pedagogical content knowledge, especially knowledge of content and teaching	Analyze video clips using guiding questions that focus on the role of the teacher

work through the problem, design a lesson incorporating the problem, teach that lesson to their students, and discuss their classroom experiences in the two subsequent workshops. For the PSC to be successful, the problem must be rich enough to foster a productive learning experience for the teachers over the course of three workshops and must be appropriate for students across grade levels (adapted as necessary). In our development and implementation of the PSC model, we have found that effective PSC problems meet the following criteria:

1. Address multiple mathematical concepts and skills
2. Are accessible to learners with different levels of mathematical knowledge
3. Have multiple entry and exit points
4. Have an imaginable context
5. Provide a foundation for productive mathematical communication
6. Are both challenging for teachers and appropriate for students

Given the current widespread adoption of the Common Core State Standards for Mathematics, it is important to use problems that address multiple objectives across the grade levels of the participating teachers.

There are a number of excellent resources on which facilitators can draw in order to select appropriate problems for their groups of teachers. The pool of relevant resources is constantly evolving and expanding, particularly as states and districts gear up for the CCSSM and associated assessments. Here, we point the interested reader to some of the resources that our team has found to be helpful. These resources include books such as *Fostering Algebraic Thinking* (Driscoll, 1999), *NCSM Great Tasks for Mathematics K–5* (Schrock et al., 2013), and *NCSM Great Tasks for Mathematics 6–12* (Schrock et al., 2013); textbooks such as *Elementary and Middle School Mathematics: Teaching Developmentally* (Van de Walle, Karp, & Bay-Williams, 2007); teacher professional development materials such as *Best Buys, Ratios and Rates* (Jacob & Fosnot, 2008) and *The Fostering Geometric Thinking Toolkit* (Driscoll et al., 2008); and online sources such as the Mathematics Assessment Project (map.mathshell.org), Illustrative Mathematics (www.illustrativemathematics.org), and Balanced Assessment in Mathematics (balancedassessment.concord.org).

Conducting the Workshop

Rather than simply providing teachers with the selected PSC problems—which are generally written with students in mind—we have found that Workshop 1 is most effective if the facilitator creates a "teacher-analysis task." One type of teacher-analysis task that we've found to be effective includes the PSC problem that will be provided to the participants' students, together with a variety of solution strategies (both correct and incorrect) that students are likely to use. The "task" is for teachers to carefully analyze each of the solution strategies—for example, thinking through which are correct or incorrect, why, and the potential gaps in students' knowledge. By focusing their attention on a given set of solution strategies, teachers can begin to anticipate how their own students might solve the problem while unpacking the critical mathematical ideas within the problem.

We generally ask teachers to first consider the analysis task individually. They then work on it collaboratively—for example, in pairs or small groups. Once teachers have had a chance to brainstorm in small groups, the facilitator typically will bring everyone together to debrief and summarize main ideas. Throughout the process, the facilitator asks questions and helps promote a deep understanding of the mathematical concepts and skills necessary to teach the problem. As the teachers work through common misconceptions, preconceptions, and incomplete understandings that students are likely to hold, they can discuss how to help students learn the key the mathematical concepts embedded in the problem.

Another type of teacher-analysis task that we have found to be effective in promoting teachers' deep understanding of the mathematics necessary to teach the PSC problem involves having the teachers work in small groups to solve the task, with each group charged to use a different representation (e.g., manipulatives, tables, and symbolic expressions). Each group produces a poster illustrating its solution strategy, and listing the pros and cons of using the representation the group was assigned. The facilitator has each group share its poster and then leads a discussion about the mathematical relationships between the different representations and solution strategies, and their relative strengths and limitations.

During the next portion of Workshop 1, the teachers design a lesson for their students focused on the PSC problem. As teachers create lesson plans tailored to their own students, they talk with their colleagues and the facilitator about issues such as their mathematical goals for students, the prior knowledge students will need for the lesson, and how they will adapt the problem to make it more accessible for their students. By the end of the workshop, teachers will have explored the mathematical opportunities presented by the problem, considered how students might attempt to solve it, and developed a concrete plan for using the problem in their classrooms.

TEACHING AND VIDEOTAPING THE PSC LESSON

Between Workshops 1 and 2, each participant teaches the problem in one of his or her mathematics classes, and the lesson is videotaped. In our projects, we used two cameras to record each lesson. One camera followed the teacher throughout the lesson, and a second camera captured a group of students as they worked during small-group activities. We gave teachers copies of their videotaped lessons, and strongly encouraged them to watch and reflect on the lesson individually. However, we have found that teachers are sometimes hesitant to watch their own lessons. Asking the teachers to select possible video clips to be discussed in Workshops 2 and 3 provides an added incentive for them to carefully review their lessons, and can help the facilitator gather a set of clips to consider in planning these workshops.

One of the most important components of Workshops 2 and 3 is the analysis of students' mathematical reasoning and teachers' pedagogical moves, prompted by the video clips of their PSC lessons. After the videotaping occurs, the facilitator selects short clips from one or more lessons to serve as anchors for discussions about learning and teaching. The set of video clips that is available for the facilitator to choose from is, of course, constrained by the number of teachers who were videotaped teaching the PSC problem. When all of the participants are videotaped, there is a wider range of clip options and a greater likelihood of finding clips that will present engaging learning opportunities.

Even when teachers nominate clips from their own lessons that may be appropriate for viewing in the upcoming workshops, the facilitator ultimately decides which clips will be shown to the whole group. Choosing clips that match the facilitator's goals for the workshops and that are likely to spur lively conversations related to those goals is essential. Therefore, we encourage the facilitator to have the final say when it comes to selecting the clips. We have incorporated periods of time into Workshops 2 and 3 where teachers work in pairs or small groups to discuss one or more clips of their choice. However, the major emphasis in these workshops is on whole-group viewing of facilitator-selected clips, as described below.

PSC WORKSHOP 2:
VIDEO ANALYSIS OF STUDENT THINKING AND INSTRUCTION

In Workshops 2 and 3, teachers share their common experience of teaching the PSC problem. The selected video clips help situate teachers' explorations in their classroom practice and foster productive discussions about teaching and learning. Both workshops highlight the mathematical reasoning that students applied to the selected problem and the mathematical practices in which they engaged while solving it, as well as the instructional skills and strategies entailed in teaching using rich problems. Typically, unpacking student thinking is emphasized in Workshop 2 and analyzing instructional strategies is emphasized in Workshop 3.

We want to note that in some of our earlier publications, we described Workshop 2 as focusing mainly on instructional practices and Workshop 3 as focusing mainly on student thinking. After several years of piloting the PSC and soliciting feedback from participants, our research team agreed that the teachers appear more comfortable engaging first in conversations related to student thinking and then in conversations about instructional practice. We have consistently maintained that these two foci are strongly linked; however, in each workshop the more salient topic can be foregrounded while the other remains in the background.

Based on our experience, we recommend that the central objectives of Workshop 2 be (1) to deepen teachers' knowledge of students' thinking about the mathematics in the selected PSC problem, and (2) to collectively generate ideas about how to foster students' mathematical reasoning. Teachers consider ways to elicit, attend to, and build on students' mathematical reasoning by studying the selected video clips and possibly other artifacts that depict student thinking. For example, teachers might share their students' written work on the PSC problem, posters created by groups of students, or their written reflections to provide a springboard for discussions of student thinking. Any of these classroom artifacts might enable the teachers to explore, for instance, unexpected solution methods and interesting ways that students explained, justified, or represented their ideas.

Planning the Workshop

When planning for Workshop 2, facilitators identify specific goals for the workshop and select video clips to situate discussions in the teachers' own classrooms. Identifying goals for the video-based discussion and selecting appropriate video clips are interrelated decisions, and either decision might precede the other in the planning process. That is, a decision about the mathematical and pedagogical goals for the discussion will naturally impact the choice of video clips. Conversely, facilitators may select a goal for the discussion because they identify particularly interesting moments in a videotaped lesson that warrant careful unpacking and deep exploration. Decisions about goals for a given workshop depend primarily on the needs and interests of the participants as well as the overall goals of the PD program.

A major task in planning Workshop 2 is selecting appropriate video clips (and perhaps other artifacts) from the teachers' PSC lessons. We have found that video clips that work well in Workshops 2 and 3 have the following characteristics:

1. They focus teachers on a particular topic that is relevant to the goal of the workshop.

2. They help the group learn something about mathematical content, student thinking, and/or instructional practices.
3. They cover a relatively short time period (typically, about 2 to 5 minutes).
4. They foster reflection and discussion.

For Workshop 2, clips portraying situations such as the following are likely to capture teachers' attention and foster productive discussions: students grappling with a mathematical concept in unique ways, students' misconceptions or erroneous solutions to the problem, and students in small groups explaining their solutions to one another.

A critical component of planning for productive video-based discussions is identifying specific aspects of the video clip that are important for teachers to notice and discuss. By identifying in advance the features of the video clip that they would like the group to analyze, facilitators can craft questions to focus the teachers' attention on those features. Guiding questions help frame teachers' conversations about each video clip, encouraging them to discuss the mathematical concepts and reasoning evident (or lacking) in the clip. It is essential for facilitators to come to the workshop with questions prepared to focus the viewing of the videos and to launch discussions. Equally important, but more often neglected in the planning process, are "back-pocket questions" that the facilitator can pull out to enliven the discussion or shift its direction. One helpful way to identify these back-pocket questions is to anticipate what the teachers are likely to notice in the video clip, what they are likely to miss, and the range of comments they might offer during the discussion. By anticipating how teachers are likely to respond to a particular clip or guiding question, facilitators can help ensure that the conversation goes down an intentional path and remains productive.

Conducting the Workshop

Workshop 2 generally begins with teachers reflecting on and sharing their experiences teaching the PSC problem. They then move into a discussion of the selected video clips and other artifacts such as students' written work, which provide concrete examples of the students' mathematical reasoning related to the problem and the mathematical practices they used in solving the problem. Close analysis of the mathematical content in the clips and other artifacts often leads the teachers to rework the problem and to engage in mathematically sophisticated conversations. For example, teachers may be prompted to discuss the pros and cons of various solution methods used by students in the clips, the progression from naïve to more formal understandings of the content, and mathematical ideas embedded in the problem that they had not previously considered.

PSC WORKSHOP 3:
VIDEO ANALYSIS OF INSTRUCTION AND STUDENT THINKING

The central purpose of the third workshop is to foster teachers' knowledge of content and teaching by guiding them to think deeply about the role they played in teaching the selected problem to their students. The majority of time in Workshop 3 is spent watching and discussing short video clips from one or more of the teachers' lessons, and exploring specific pedagogical activities such as launching the lesson, guiding students as they work in small groups, or leading a whole-class discussion about multiple solution strategies. The workshop provides teachers with the opportunity to critically reflect on their own instructional practices, along with those of their colleagues, as they analyze video clips and participate in guided discussions. The rich problem and accompanying video situate the workshop within specific mathematical content and classroom practices, and this interaction between content and pedagogy is highlighted throughout the workshop.

Planning the Workshop

In planning for Workshop 3, the facilitator identifies one or more aspects of the teacher's role for the group to explore. This decision is likely to be based on the facilitator's knowledge of the teachers' classroom practices, their specific interests with respect to improving learning and instruction, and contextual factors such as the goals of their particular school or district. Facilitators we worked with have chosen to focus on topics such as introducing the problem; posing questions to elicit, challenge, and extend students' thinking; deciding when to provide explanations, ask leading questions, or let students follow their own line of reasoning; and wrapping up the lesson. In keeping with these foci, they selected video clips that depict situations such as an interaction in which the teacher attempts to understand a student's approach to solving the problem; different adaptations of the problem to address particular learning goals; and different ways to introduce the problem or draw the activity to a close. To select video clips and create guiding and back-pocket questions, facilitators consider the same characteristics they did in planning for Workshop 2, but with an emphasis on instructional practices.

Conducting the Workshop

During the workshop, teachers view the selected clips and engage in guided conversations about the instructional episodes the clips capture. Often, a video clip is viewed multiple times, as the conversation suggests another perspective to take or another interpretation to explore. Teachers may discuss, for example, how specific instructional moves supported or constrained student thinking, or how different ways of launching the lesson influenced the solution strategies they pursued. Teachers are also encouraged to think critically about their classroom implementation of the PSC problem and consider ways they would modify their future planning and implementation of that problem, as well as more general instructional improvements they might seek to make.

Workshop 3 also includes time for teachers to reflect on what they have learned over the course of that iteration of the PSC. As they reflect, individually (in writing) and/or collaboratively (in small- or whole-group discussions), the teachers not only consider how they might change their instructional practices based on the knowledge they have gained thus far, but also provide valuable input to the facilitator that can be used to shape future PSC workshops.

SUCCESSIVE ITERATIONS OF THE PSC

The PSC model is designed to support long-term professional learning in which teachers engage in successive iterations of PSC workshops. A single iteration of the PSC typically corresponds to an academic semester, which means that teachers can participate in two iterations per school year. As they participate in multiple cycles of the PSC, teachers have the opportunity to gain new insights and continually add to their knowledge base. Each iteration is unique. Over time, the goals and focus are likely to shift, teachers will become more familiar and comfortable with the model, and facilitators will gain more experience as PSC leaders. Cycles of the PSC build on one another and capitalize on teachers' expanding knowledge, interests, and sense of community. In our own implementation of the PSC, we have found that as teachers' knowledge, analytic skills, and community strengthen, facilitators can probe more deeply into relevant and challenging ideas.

The PSC model does not come with specifications as to which content areas or topics should be covered. Depending on the local context, facilitators may decide to traverse a specified mathematical terrain over a given period of time, such as a content area in the Common Core State Standards that they recognize as particularly challenging for their group. In addition, facilitators may elect to highlight certain pedagogical topics, such as one or more of the CCSS mathematical practice standards. For example, a facilitator might select a mathematical problem that is aligned with specific content standards and ask teachers to carefully consider selected practice standards when they plan for, teach, and analyze videos related to that problem. In subsequent iterations of the PSC, facilitators might select another problem that is connected to different but related content standards, and continue to target the same practice standards. It is well documented that professional development that is sustained over time is more likely to lead to the types of outcomes that districts, principals, and teachers themselves value—that is, increased learning opportunities for both teachers and students.

PROFESSIONAL LEARNING IN DISTRICT, SCHOOL, OR GRADE-LEVEL GROUPS

We have implemented the PSC with different configurations of teacher groups. In some cases, the teachers come together from different school districts, sometimes they are all from the same district, sometimes they are colleagues from within the same school, and sometimes they are teachers who work at the same grade level (either within or across schools). Bringing together teachers with a wide range of perspectives and instructional experiences can be challenging but at the same time extremely powerful. As part of the PSC model, all of the participating teachers implement the same problem—most often, across a variety of grade levels. Although teachers are encouraged to find ways to modify the problem and differentiate instruction for diverse groups of students, a central component of participating in a PSC group is that the teachers share a common instructional experience. The experience then serves as a basis for the group of teachers to communicate and connect with one another in ways that are unlikely to occur without the common experience.

Some of the teachers we have worked with initially expressed reluctance to use problems they perceived to be outside of their curriculum or intended for students at a different grade level. However, once the participants experience an iteration or two of the PSC, they generally begin to appreciate the unique learning opportunities that come from exploring a focal mathematical concept that spans multiple grade levels and promotes discussions regarding vertical articulation. We have also found that explicitly connecting the problem to specific standards helps alleviate the teachers' concerns. For example, we had teachers modify a PSC problem focused on unit rate and connect it to the CCSSM standards at each middle school grade level. The 6th-grade teachers generated lesson plans based on finding the unit rate in tables, 7th-grade teachers emphasized finding the constant proportionality or unit rate in tables, and 8th-grade teachers encouraged their students to explore proportional relationships and interpret unit rate as the slope of a graph.

THE DEGREE OF FLEXIBILITY BUILT INTO THE PSC

As we have mentioned throughout the chapter, the PSC is designed to be an adaptive, flexible model of mathematics PD. Built into the model are numerous options and decisions that facilitators can make to ensure that the model is the right fit for their teachers. Facilitators can decide, for example, how many workshops to hold in each iteration of the PSC, the duration of each workshop, what the focus of the workshops should be (in terms of content and learning goals), and which video clips to select to match their goals. At the same time, the PSC does have parameters, and stepping outside of certain boundaries may mean that facilitators are not being true to the intentions and design of the model.

To carry out an iteration of the PSC as intended, facilitators should maintain the following aspects of the model:

- Organize a group of teachers who work on a designated mathematical problem.
- At least some of the teachers should use the problem with their own students.
- At least some of the teachers should be videotaped as they use the problem.
- The teachers discuss their experiences and view video clips from their own classrooms.

We anticipate that some groups of teachers will engage in a variation of this process. For example, teachers within a group may work on different mathematical problems, or may simply discuss their experiences and perhaps bring in examples of student work rather than being videotaped. These variations are certainly understandable and may be quite appropriate given the group's circumstances. However, we would argue that they are far enough removed from the core of the PSC model that the teachers are no longer truly engaging in the PSC. In some cases, facilitators may decide that they need to start with these types of adaptations and gradually move closer to the core components of the PSC. Or, conversely, they may start by using the PSC as we have defined it and then move further away from the core elements as dictated by their unique needs and circumstances.

Working with districts, schools, and teachers involves a wide range of moving parts and frequent change in resources, personnel, and goals. The PSC model, to a large degree, is premised on adaptability and flexibility. As designers, we cannot foresee all the potential variations that may arise. For the most part, the nature of these variations is less important than the intentions behind them. As long as there is a clear focus on supporting sustained teacher and student learning in a meaningful way, we are confident that the PD will be an impactful, positive experience.

CHAPTER 3

The PSC Model in Action

To give the reader a feel for what it is like to participate in the PSC, in this chapter we present vignettes derived from actual PSC workshops that were videotaped as part of our research. The vignettes are short descriptions that are meant to briefly but authentically depict the events and conversations that took place during a given workshop. The vignettes come from three workshops, or one cycle of the PSC, using the Disc Problem (adapted from Schwartz & Kenney, 1995; the problem will be described in detail as the chapter progresses). Pseudonyms are used for all teachers, students, and schools mentioned in this book.

The facilitator of these Disc Problem workshops is Kaitlyn, a mathematics teacher and chair of the mathematics department at Four Reed Middle School. At the time she conducted the workshops, Kaitlyn had 19 years of experience as a mathematics teacher. As the department chair, Kaitlyn was responsible for leading monthly meetings with the other mathematics teachers in her school, during which they engaged in activities such as discussing a selected book they had all read and mapping their curriculum to the current state standards. Having recently completed a 1-week Summer Leadership Academy focused on learning to facilitate the PSC (see Chapter 6), the Disc Problem workshops were Kaitlyn's first efforts at facilitating the PSC.

A WINDOW INTO WORKSHOP 1:
UNPACKING THE MATHEMATICS IN THE DISC PROBLEM

In addition to Kaitlyn, there are six mathematics teachers at Four Reed Middle School. After attending a workshop orienting them to the PSC, five of the six teachers have elected to participate in the PD. On the designated date, after school, these five teachers come to Kaitlyn's classroom and seat themselves at desks arranged in a group near the front of the room. Along with Kaitlyn there are three female teachers (Gina, Terri, and Rachel) and two male teachers (Kevin and John). A feeling of camaraderie is evident as the teachers immediately engage in small talk as they settle into their seats. They discuss issues they are currently facing in the school and with their students, and also provide updates about events in their personal lives. After a few minutes, Kaitlyn moves to the center of the room and assumes a more formal tone as she begins the workshop.

Kaitlyn tells the group, "As you know, today we are starting the Problem-Solving Cycle. The problem we'll be using is pretty unique. When I first saw it, I thought it was kind of 'out there,' but I think it is going to be fun for you. It's called the Disc Problem. I taught it to my own students last week."

Kaitlyn then reads the beginning portion of the Disc Problem, which she also shows as a PowerPoint slide projected on the whiteboard: "A can of soup, a coin, and a piece of spaghetti are all cylinders even though they look very different. One might say the coin is more disc-like than the spaghetti."

Kaitlyn holds up a piece of spaghetti and a penny and continues, "I brought in some spaghetti so we can look at it. As you can see, the coin is more disc-like than the spaghetti, and the spaghetti is more like a cylinder. So you might ask yourself: What is a cylinder? What is a disc? Is a cylinder a disc? Is a disc a cylinder?"

Kaitlyn instructs the group to take a few minutes to think about these questions and jot down some initial ideas.

As the teachers begin writing, Kaitlyn places a variety of cylindrical objects on their desks. Some teachers work quietly, while others want to discuss their ideas and are more boisterous. After about 4 minutes, Kaitlyn brings the group together to share their thoughts.

Kevin offers, "I thought about the differences between the spaghetti and coin that you held up. I actually thought about the height compared to the diameter. In my mind, a cylinder has a greater height than diameter. The penny, for example, has a height that is smaller than the diameter, so it would be a disc. The poster tube, where the height is clearly more than the diameter, would be a cylinder."

"But," Gina responds, "I think you have to have a disc to have a cylinder and a cylinder to have a disc. I think they're related. One is the same as the other."

Rachel agrees, "I, too, thought they were the same thing."

However, John has a different opinion: "I don't think a cylinder is a disc. I think that a disc is a cylinder but a cylinder does not have to be a disc."

Gina jumps back into the conversation animatedly and explains her idea further: "Yes, but I went back to the definition I wrote, which was: 'A cylinder is a 3-D shape that's round with a circular base and has a height.' A disc also has height, but it is a minimal height. I do think the definitions are basically the same."

Kaitlyn does not attempt to resolve the controversy surrounding the teachers' definitions. She recognizes that the group is thinking deeply about important mathematical issues and decides they are ready to move forward. Defining what a disc is, in relation to a cylinder, lies at the heart of the problem and is a topic they will continue to revisit over the course of the workshop.

Kaitlyn shows the next PowerPoint slide, which contains the complete Disc Problem (see Figure 3.1). The teachers appear excited and intrigued as they read over the problem and notice its ambiguities. Kaitlyn briefly talks through each of the steps listed in the problem and then gives the teachers 15 minutes to work on it.

In PSC Workshop 1, teachers gather as an informal community of practice, engaging in a rich mathematical problem and a teacher-analysis task based on the problem. Once the facilitator launches the selected PSC problem, teachers carefully consider the mathematics in the problem and work to arrive at a solution. In this case, Kaitlyn's launch involves having the teachers generate and discuss definitions of the terms *cylinder* and *disc*, which helps them develop some shared language as well as a sense of the complexity of the topic before actively beginning to solve the problem. PSC facilitators strive to model effective pedagogy and promote discussions that allow for a myriad of ideas to emerge, including different interpretations of the problem and a range of solution strategies. In this way, teachers experience a supportive learning community as they confront the intricacies of the problem at hand.

Once the teachers have worked on the Disc Problem in small groups for approximately 15 minutes, Kaitlyn brings them back together so they can share their thinking. Kaitlyn inquires, "Does anyone want to tell us about how you approached the problem?"

Kevin responds, "I can start and describe what John and I did. You know how earlier I said that height and diameter are really the whole focus of this

Figure 3.1. The Disc Problem

1. Given the variety of cylinders you have in front of you, devise a definition of disc-ness that allows you to say which object is the most disc-like and which is the least.
2. Write a formula (or algorithm or algebraic sentence) that expresses your measure of disc-ness. You may introduce any labels and definitions you like and use all the mathematical language you care to.
3. Make any measurements you need, and calculate a numerical value of disc-ness for each of the six items.
4. Discuss whether these numbers seem reasonable in light of your definition of disc-ness.
5. How would you change your answers to these questions if you were asked to write a formula for cylinder-ness rather than disc-ness?

problem? [Other teachers nod in confirmation.] John and I decided to define a disc as an object where the diameter is greater than the height. Then I just came up straight away with the formulas. For disc-ness I said you would calculate diameter over height, as a ratio. And in that sense, the greater the number, the more disc-like it is. For example, this can had a diameter-to-height ratio of 1.95, whereas this penny had a diameter-to-height ratio of 10. I would say that the penny is much more disc-like. As long as the ratio is greater than 1, we'll call it a disc. And if it is less than 1, we'll call it a cylinder. The roll of pennies had a ratio of .25, so we're calling that a cylinder."

Kaitlyn probes, "So if the ratio of diameter to height is exactly 1, what is it?"

Kevin replies with a laugh, "Yeah, that is where we got into that weird gray area. We called it a discylinder." [The group laughs.]

John comments, "I would like to see what an object with a ratio of 1 would look like. That would be interesting in terms of teaching the problem."

Kaitlyn prompts the group, "How could you bring up this idea when working with your students?"

Kevin answers, "We could use pennies and stack them one at a time until the diameter is equal to the height."

Rachel offers some other strategies: "We could have them cut strips of paper and make their own cylinders. Or we can try to find a can that has equal dimensions."

Kaitlyn asks the group if they have any other ideas for how to measure disc-ness.

Gina answers, "Terri, Rachel, and I did a comparison of diameter and height. We determined that if the diameter is greater than the height, the object will be more disc-like. But if the diameter is less than the height, it will be more cylinder-like."

In this discussion, right from the start Kevin repeats his definition of a disc. Kevin and John then offer a ratio-based formula that will enable them to calculate the "disc-ness" of various objects. Gina, Rachel, and Terri provide an alternative approach. Although their formula also incorporates the variables of diameter and height, the relationship between these two variables is presented as an inequality rather than as a ratio. They will soon recognize that looking only at which variable is greater (diameter versus height) has important limitations, including the fact that it does not allow them to calculate a value for the "disc-ness" of an object or determine which of two objects is more disc-like. However, their line of thinking is certainly reasonable, and it is common among middle schoolers who are presented with the Disc Problem.

After the teachers have shared their solution strategies, Kaitlyn shows the group a teacher-analysis task for the Disc Problem, which lists six strategies that might be offered by middle school students (see Figure 3.2). Kaitlyn asks the teachers to think about each strategy, decide whether it is viable, and consider why or why not. Shifting the conversation to a focus

Figure 3.2. Teacher-Analysis Task for the Disc Problem: Six Student Strategies

1. Let the radius of the disc be R and height be h, then subtract R–h.
2. Let the diameter of the disc be D and the height be h, then subtract D–h. When the number is 0 or positive, the object is a disc. The higher the number, the more disc-like the object. All negative numbers are cylinders or less disc-like. The number furthest from 0 is the most cylindrical.
3. 0.9 for the tuna-fish can, 6.3 for the coin, 0.3 for the soup can, 0.08 for the mailing tube, 0.01 for the straw, and 0.003 for the spaghetti.
4. When D > h, the object is a disc.
5. When the circumference > h, the object is more disc-like.
6. D:h. If the ratio is 1 or greater than 1, the object is a disc. If the ratio is less than 1, the object is a cylinder.

on student strategies encourages the teachers to delve deeply into the mathematical content and, at the same time, to consider how students in their own classes might approach the problem and how they might support their students to be successful with the problem.

Referring back to how they originally approached the problem, Kaitlyn tells Kevin and John, "If you notice, the answer that you just shared with us is listed as strategy number 6." She then turns to Gina, Rachel, and Terri, and says, "Your answer is number 4."

The teachers then discuss among themselves each of the strategies. They begin to measure the cans and other objects placed on their desks to make sense of and test the different ways of thinking listed in the teacher-analysis task. After about 15 minutes have passed, Kaitlyn leads a group discussion focused on what the teachers have discovered about the ways students might think about the Disc Problem.

Kevin begins, "Well, the first two strategies are difference models, where you are subtracting. So they do not work." The other teachers nod in agreement.

John continues, "The other four strategies can be interpreted as comparison models. The last one is an ideal strategy, involving the use of a ratio."

Gina wonders, "In number 1, they are taking the radius and subtracting the height. A negative number would get you a cylinder. Is there a case where that rule doesn't work? Where you would get a negative number, but not want to classify the object as a cylinder?"

Terri responds, "Well, if the radius was 3 and the height was 4, the difference would be -1. But if we use the diameter, the diameter would be 6. So 6 minus 4 gives us positive 2. Given the same object, if we use the radius we get a negative number, which means it's a cylinder. But then if we use the diameter we get a positive number, which means it's a disc."

Kaitlyn prompts the teachers to talk more about strategy number 2. John replies, "Well, it is better than using the radius. But the statement 'the number furthest away from zero is the most cylindrical' is a problem. A Frisbee would have a value much further away from zero than a can of soup, but the Frisbee is clearly more disc-like than the soup."

Kaitlyn moves on to strategy number 3.

Rachel offers, "I think what the numbers represent are the values of disc-ness that you get from using the ratio of diameter to height. It is the same as number 6, just without the formula."

Kaitlyn affirms this idea and follows up by asking, "So with a proportion, we can get a calculated value of disc-ness. Can we do that with the difference models or inequalities such as numbers 4 and 5?"

The teachers think for a moment, and then Kevin replies, "I see that now. With the difference equations and inequality statements, they are not formulas that you can use to generate a value for the disc-ness of an object. We're really going to have to help our students recognize the power of using a proportional relationship!"

Working through the teacher-analysis task enables the teachers to compare and contrast a variety of potential solutions to the Disc Problem, including difference models (additive strategies), inequalities, and ratios (multiplicative strategies). Their conversation is typical of conversations that commonly occur at this point in Workshop 1, serving to deepen the teachers' mathematical knowledge for teaching. For instance, Terri points out a relatively subtle issue with the two additive strategies, noticing that for some objects the formula using radius produces the opposite answer of the formula using diameter given the rationale stated for strategy 2. Additionally, analyzing a range of strategies helps teachers anticipate how their own students might approach the problem, leading to a more informed consideration of how to support their students in learning the important concepts. After this examination of the mathematical ideas entailed in each strategy, Kaitlyn segues into lesson planning.

Kaitlyn tells the group, "This is a weird problem in that *disc-ness* is not a real word. But using this word and this idea in the problem can produce good mathematical conversations on the concept of ratio. You know, helping kids consider the diameter and height of different objects, how those variables are related to each other, and how we can use them to figure out ways to compare the items. What I want you to think about now is: How will your kids react to this problem?"

Gina clarifies, "So, the expectation is that students will come up with a strategy to try to figure out if each object is a disc or a cylinder. And in particular how they can do that mathematically?"

Kaitlyn replies, "Yes. My hope is that students would come up with the idea of using a ratio or proportion because that shows a deep understanding of relationships and comparisons. That said, I have taught this problem in two classes and not one student has come up with a ratio, although some have come up with one dimension being greater than the other. You need to decide on specific learning goals, how you will present the problem to your students, and how you will support them."

John queries his fellow teachers, "Are you guys planning to bring in items like these, or do you want to give them paper to cut and make into different sized cylinders?"

Gina replies, "I think I would rather give them specific objects. And then have them test their theory with paper."

Terri adds, "I like using the cans and other cylinders. It makes the problem more realistic and they like to measure. I think with my 6th-graders I will guide them to measure and then look at the comparisons."

Kaitlyn offers, "When I first taught the problem, I just said 'come up with a formula and then test it.' They had blank faces, and were totally confused by that. So for my second class I changed it and gave them the option to start either way—with a formula or with measuring."

An important point that Kaitlyn tries to get across is that the teachers have a great deal of flexibility to implement the Disc Problem as they see fit in their own classrooms. Kaitlyn offers her own experiences using the problem to help the other teachers in her group develop realistic expectations for their students' work, to prompt them to develop mathematical learning goals for their students, and to encourage them to carefully consider their introduction of the problem.

As Workshop 1 draws to a close, the teachers finish developing their individual lesson plans and excitedly discuss the different approaches they have in mind. They acknowledge, for example, that Gina needs to make instructional decisions for her sixth-grade class that are different from the decisions made by Rachel, who is teaching Algebra I. As the teachers leave the workshop, they tell Kaitlyn that they are looking forward to seeing how these differences play out and will report back when they meet in a few weeks for Workshop 2.

WINDOWS INTO WORKSHOPS 2 AND 3:
VIDEO ANALYSIS OF THE DISC PROBLEM

Kaitlyn's main emphasis for PSC Workshops 2 and 3 is on encouraging her group of teachers to examine students' mathematical thinking and reflect on their own instructional practice, within the context of the Disc Problem. In this cycle, she elects to foreground teachers' instructional practice during Workshop 2 and students' thinking during Workshop 3. (As we described in Chapter 2, PSC facilitators have flexibility in determining which topic to foreground first.) In both workshops, Kaitlyn's group spends the majority of their time watching and discussing video clips, along with a consideration of selected lesson artifacts.

When planning Workshop 2, Kaitlyn decided to use video clips from Gina's lesson to highlight instruction on proportional reasoning. As we will see in the vignette drawn from that workshop, watching and discussing videos serves to slow down the act of teaching and enables the group to narrow in on specific teacher moves, alternative options, and their affordances and constraints relative to student learning. For Workshop 3, Kaitlyn elected to show clips from her own classroom. Although Kaitlyn's main emphasis is on students' mathematical thinking, the workshop also prompts the group to think in new ways about the Disc Problem—especially mathematical components of the problem that they have not previously addressed and ideas for improving their instruction in the future.

Workshop 2

About a month after Workshop 1, the teachers meet again for Workshop 2. Kaitlyn begins by talking openly about some of her own frustrations in using the Disc Problem, particularly the fact that most of her students did not get to a ratio strategy. Her opening sets the tone and focus for the workshop, which emphasizes honest and reflective communication and brainstorming instructional moves that will help students shift from additive to multiplicative thinking.

Kaitlyn begins the workshop by asking the teachers to write down some reflections on using the Disc Problem in their classrooms. After a few minutes, they share their answers as a whole group. Gina begins, "I told my students the day before I taught this lesson that the problem has more than one answer. This group of kids is so set on just getting the right answer that I think having them grapple with the ambiguity of the problem was really good."

Terri adds, "I think that the discussion at the beginning of my lesson went really well, when we were talking about the objects and which were more cylinder-like or more disc-like. They got excited about it. I think having props really helped. But knowing what to do with the props is where I lost them."

Kaitlyn sympathizes with Terri and notes, "I left the problem very open-ended because I was using the lesson as a pre-assessment of where my students are with 3-D objects and the vocabulary related to that topic. I had one student who threw a bunch of vocabulary at me, and it was obvious that she had no idea what the words meant. So I made a mental note that she would need help later on. I did get some formulas, and some recognition of a relationship between diameter and height. I thought that was good, but I was not really satisfied with the outcome."

Terri comments optimistically, "I have some ideas of what I would like to do differently the next time I teach the problem. I would give them information on ratio and proportion and ask them to use that information to decide whether something is more cylinder-like or disc-like."

Kaitlyn inquires, "So you would use the word *ratio*?"

Terri replies, "Yes, I think so. I had management issues with the kids breaking the spaghetti and acting up, and that is not like these kids. I think they just had no idea what to do. So next time, I would put the idea of ratio out there first. I think I would also give them a chart with headings because my kids looked at the blank chart and had no idea what to do with it. I would guide them more."

Kaitlyn smiles and moves into watching a video clip, "So, while some of us did not get our students to think of a ratio solution, Gina did! We are going to watch a clip from Gina's class to see how she guided student thinking. We'll watch one clip—a 2-minute portion of her lesson—where the students begin to realize that a ratio might help them determine how disc-like an object is. I think her lesson is pretty exciting and we will learn a lot from these clips."

The fact that Kaitlyn candidly talks about the struggles she encountered in teaching the Disc Problem to her 8th-grade students seems to foster a safe and supportive community. Kaitlyn's openness encourages the other teachers to bring up aspects of their teaching practice that seem problematic to them, with the goal of learning from their own mistakes and from their colleagues. The teachers clearly recognize that there are numerous pedagogical choices involved in teaching the Disc Problem, and beginning with this initial reflective activity, during Workshop 2 they actively consider different options that they might have used or that they plan to use in the future.

After the teachers have shared their reflections, Kaitlyn frames Gina's video clip as stemming from an effective pedagogical choice, ultimately leading the students to be successful with this challenging problem. By first highlighting the complexity of teaching the Disc Problem, and then presenting Gina's clip as one from which the group can learn, Kaitlyn sets the stage for a productive and in-depth analysis of instructional practice.

Kaitlyn turns to Gina and asks, "Will you set up the clip and talk about how you taught the lesson?"

Gina explains, "I introduced the problem and had the students work in groups. I had them use the cylinders at their desks and order them from least disc-like to most disc-like. Most of my kids understood that they needed to look at diameter and height."

Kaitlyn adds, "She also did a nice job at the end of the lesson, bringing the students back together and having each group share. Gina had written all of the students' solutions on the whiteboard, and they went over each one as a class to figure out how each group derived its formula. You will see it worked really well."

Kaitlyn reminds the teachers about the "norms" for watching video, emphasizing that the purpose is to spark inquiry around pedagogical moves, including moves that are and are not evident in the video. Then the group watches the clip, in which Gina is sharing a student's use of the subtraction method:

> With Gina's prompting, a student, Sally, talks to the class about her method: "We determined that if d – h > 0, it is a disc. And if you have d – h < 0, it is a cylinder."
>
> Standing at the front of the room, Gina asks the class to react to Sally's method. "What do you all think? Does anyone have anything else to say about the subtraction method?"
>
> After a period of silence, one student offers, "I think that it works to tell you whether the object is a disc or a cylinder." There is more silence, and no one else responds.
>
> Gina holds up a CD and a penny. She continues to probe: "What if I am comparing this CD with this penny? Is one more disc-like than the other? How does the subtraction solution help you figure that out?"
>
> Elliott responds that although Sally's formula is good for identifying whether objects are discs or cylinders, it does not answer the question of which object is more disc-like. For example, they can't use the formula to tell whether a penny or a CD is more disc-like.
>
> Gina nods her head in agreement and follows up by asking, "So, how can you determine the disc-ness of objects?"
>
> One student suggests, "Well, you could compare the diameter and height as a ratio."
>
> Gina excitedly encourages the class, "Why don't you think about this idea and see what you can find out?"

The video clip shows Gina questioning her students about two objects that both are clearly discs: a CD and a penny. By asking which object is *more* disc-like, Gina helps her students to see that Sally's strategy only allows for the classification of objects as discs or cylinders. In order to determine the relative disc-ness of objects, the students will need to come up with a different method. After watching Gina's clip twice, Kaitlyn encourages the teachers to brainstorm other ways they can help students shift from a reliance on additive strategies to more powerful ratio strategies.

John suggests, "You could use some type of object that has a ratio of 1. That would press students to think about the midpoint on a continuum from cylinder-like to disc-like."

Terri says, "I like that idea. I would also make a chart to help them organize their information about variables like diameter, height, and possibly circumference. I'd have to think about what to include. But a chart might help them see patterns and relationships, including a ratio of 1."

John continues, "I like the idea of having a variety of objects on the continuum so that they have the opportunity to discover the limitations of just subtracting. I would ask them how they can discriminate between more cylinder-like objects and more disc-like objects."

Kaitlyn adds, "I also think Terri's idea of providing them with a chart that has the headings listed would work well. I think that may be especially helpful for our 6th-grade students to get them started."

Kevin wonders aloud whether the formula d/h > 1 represents the best cutoff between discs and cylinders, as they had agreed on in Workshop 1. He asserts, "When I look at a stack of pennies with a ratio of 1, I feel that it is more of a cylinder than a disc. I'm wondering if we should rethink our formula." Kevin starts stacking pennies and then questions whether using radius in the formula instead of diameter would better reflect their shared understanding of disc-ness.

The group discusses Kevin's idea of r/h > 1 and they agree that it might be a slightly better formula. However, they acknowledge that the focus of the Disc Problem should be on supporting proportional thinking and that both formulas would work well if their students came up with them. In fact, they noted, if students happened to identify both formulas, then that could lead into a productive mathematical debate.

In line with Kaitlyn's expectations, Gina's video clip serves as a springboard for a rich discussion regarding instructional approaches that can help students make the difficult transition from additive to multiplicative thinking. The teachers recognize, for example, that encouraging students to think about the objects as falling along a continuum of disc-ness would likely support more nuanced thinking. The group also reconsiders the original solution to the problem (diameter/height) and further speculates on an appropriate cutoff between a cylinder and a disc. As the workshop comes to an end, several teachers indicate that they plan to try the Disc Problem with another one of their math classes.

Workshop 3

About 6 weeks later, the teachers come together again for Workshop 3. Kaitlyn has recently taught the Disc Problem to a different class of students, and she is excited to share some of their strategies. Kaitlyn hopes to engage the teachers in a conversation about her students' use of a ratio not only to solve the problem, but also to more deeply explore the boundaries between discs and cylinders. Kaitlyn greets the teachers as they enter her classroom and pulls up the video clip on her computer.

Kaitlyn tells the group, "Today we are going to discuss the Disc Problem for the last time, and we are going to focus on students' thinking about the mathematics. We will be looking at two different video clips of students from my 8th-grade Geometry class. I decided to teach this lesson again to a new set of students, bringing in some of the ideas that we talked about in our last workshop. My mathematical learning goal was for the students to use proportional reasoning to compare the disc-ness of different objects. I think the difference between how the lesson went with my Geometry class compared to my Math 8 class was pretty remarkable. Do you guys remember when Terri discussed creating a chart to help her students get started with the problem? [Teachers nod in confirmation.] Well, I created a spreadsheet for my students." Kaitlyn explains that she brought in six objects for her students to measure, and she had students put the objects in order from the most cylinder-like to the most disc-like, building on a suggestion by John.

Kaitlyn shares with the group, "I added a few new elements to my lesson plan that I think really helped the students think proportionally. You may notice these elements in the video clips that I'm going to share. In the first short clip, you will see two of my students, Dave and Naomi, talking to the class about what their group has been doing. I want you guys to try and figure out what Dave and Naomi were thinking."

Kaitlyn shows a 1-minute clip from the second day of a 2-day Disc Problem lesson with her students. The students have identified a formula, and they are beginning to explore the application of their formula to a variety of objects, including poker chips stacked to various heights. In the clip, Kaitlyn asks two students, Naomi and Dave, to share their group's formula and tell the class what relationships they were looking at among the cylinders.

> Naomi begins, "Our formula to determine if an object is more disc-like or more cylinder-like is D/h. So we divided the diameter by the height. And if the ratio was 1 or greater than 1, we knew it was a disc. If the ratio was less than 1, it was a cylinder. Once we figured that out, we started to think about other shapes that have the same 'body type.'"
>
> Dave continues, "Yeah, our group thinks the tuna can is a disc. But we are trying to figure out if we can use the poker chips to create an object that has the same body type as the tuna can, so we can 'see' what that might look like and check if the ratio is the same as the tuna can."

The teachers elect to watch this clip three times, in order to fully grasp what is taking place. Then, before they engage in a detailed analysis of the videotaped students' thinking, Kaitlyn distributes copies of the work completed by Naomi and Dave's group (see Figure 3.3). Naomi and Dave's group filled in one table where they recorded the diameter, radius, height, and ratio of diameter to height for six objects. On another table, they recorded the same measurements for stacks of poker chips. Kaitlyn explains that she encouraged the use of poker chips as a way for her students to explore changes in the objects' relationships when one dimension (diameter) was kept constant.

The teachers take some time to talk in pairs about the video clip as well as the tables the students completed before Kaitlyn says, "Okay, let's come back together now. What were Naomi and Dave thinking? How did they get to the point where they were in the clip?"

John answers, "It seems like they understand that a ratio is the way to determine whether a figure is more disc-like or more cylinder-like."

Terri continues, "I think they were trying to reconcile what they saw. You know, what the tuna can looked like versus the numbers in the chart for

Figure 3.3. Naomi and Dave's Tables

Item	Diameter (mm)	Radius (mm)	Height (mm)	D/H*
Penny	19	9.5	1	19
Poker Chip	35	17.5	2	17.5
Frisbee	227	113.5	30	7.57
Tuna Can	101	50.5	57	1.77
Soup Can	74	37	113	0.65
Oats Canister	102	51	176	0.58

Number of Poker Chips	Diameter (mm)	Radius (mm)	Height (mm)	D/H
1	35	17.5	2	17.5
2	35	17.5	4	8.75
3	35	17.5	6	5.83
4	35	17.5	8	4.38
5	35	17.5	10	3.50
6	35	17.5	12	2.92
7	35	17.5	14	2.50
8	35	17.5	16	2.19
9	35	17.5	18	1.94
10	35	17.5	20	1.75
11	35	17.5	22	1.59

*This quantity can be considered to be dimensionless or as millimeters of diameter per millimeters of height.

the poker chips. If they could figure out what a stack of poker chips looked like that had the same ratio as one of the objects they originally measured, it would help them feel more confident in their formula for whether something is more disc-like or cylinder-like."

John agrees, "I think you are right."

Kaitlyn directs the teachers to look carefully at Naomi and Dave's tables and specifically to notice that the stack of 10 poker chips has a diameter-to-height ratio of 1.75, which is very close to the ratio of 1.77 for the tuna can. Because of the approximate equality of these two ratios, Naomi and Dave began to wonder if the figures had the same "body type" or, in more mathematical terms, if they were similar figures. The teachers quickly calculate that indeed, the scale factor between the 10 poker chips and the tuna can is about 2.9, and they can be understood as (almost) mathematically similar. That is, the tuna can is, more or less, three times the size of the poker chips. The teachers are impressed with Dave and Naomi's proportional thinking, especially their use of a ratio to compare objects and determine not only the objects' disc-ness but also the objects' mathematical similarity.

Kaitlyn comments, "I thought it was great that the kids experimented with ideas so closely related to similarity, and it was very exciting to see their depth of understanding increase over the 2-day lesson. Now, let's shift to thinking about the best cutoff point between discs and cylinders. My students had a number of different ideas along these lines. Remember how at the end of Workshop 2 we came to the conclusion that r/h > 1 might be the best formula for establishing the cutoff point? I want to show you a second video clip that focuses on Ben and Calisha's group and their thinking about this topic, which is different from anything we have discussed so far."

> Two students, Ben and Calisha, walk to the front of the classroom in order to present their group's solution strategy.
>
> Ben starts, "For our disc-ness formula, we found the circumference of an object and divided that by the height. If the ratio is less than pi, then it's a cylinder, and if it is greater than pi, then it's a disc."
>
> Calisha adds, "At first we decided that if the ratio was 3.14, then it's a cylinder. But then we agreed it really could be either a disc or a cylinder."

Kaitlyn asks the teachers, "So what do you think of their strategy? They are looking at circumference divided by height, and their cutoff point is pi. Is that a viable option?"

Terri answers, "Yes. I think it is a very interesting way to think about the cylinders. It works for me."

John jumps in, "I agree. It's cool that they thought to use circumference."

Kevin questions, "I'm curious, how did you handle this situation in the classroom, Kaitlyn?"

Kaitlyn laughingly responds, "Well, that's the question that I wanted to ask you! So here we have one group of students arguing for a cutoff of 1.0 based on the ratio of diameter to height. Then another group argues it should be 3.14 using circumference to height. A third group says that we should just go with a cutoff of 2 because that's roughly in the middle of the other two numbers. I find it interesting how all these ideas compare with what we came up with in Workshop 2—which was that the radius divided by the height should be greater than one for the object to be a disc. Take a few minutes and talk to the person next to you about how you would facilitate a classroom conversation based on these different student solutions."

The teachers talk about the importance of accepting all strategies, noting the learning that could come from having the students debate and justify their ideas. Kaitlyn reminds the group that the two video clips she showed in this workshop are of her advanced geometry students, who quickly and comfortably went to a ratio strategy. She urges the teachers to consider both more and less advanced students, and how to promote their proportional thinking.

Kaitlyn uses Workshop 3 as an opportunity to encourage the teachers to think not only about student reasoning but about instructional practice as well. After seeing a wide variety of student approaches to the Disc Problem, the teachers continue to ponder elements of effective practice, including how to use the problem with students at different ability levels. As they share the ways they modified the Disc Problem, along with students' reactions to these modifications, the teachers brainstorm additional changes that they would make in the future and hypothesize how those changes might impact their students.

Kevin shares how he taught the Disc Problem to a group of 6th-graders: "We primarily used poker chips. They had to determine where in the stack of poker chips the cutoff was for a disc versus a cylinder. I had several groups come up with the diameter-to-height idea, but other groups I just had to lead there because they could not think of a ratio right away. I tried to make the lesson useful to the students. What I am thinking now is that I would have specific items for them to look at, and do more upfront work to prepare them."

Kaitlyn seconds the idea of preparing students more before they enter into the Disc Problem. "I would suggest providing terminology also. Even with my geometry class, I threw out the terms—*circumference, height, diameter*, and so on—instead of just saying 'go measure.' I thought that might be useful. In my Math 8 class, they did not know the terms, so that can be a big issue."

Rachel remarks, "I really like the way Kaitlyn introduced this lesson to her geometry students. Now having thought about it, I realize that I was too open-ended and just threw the problem out there. I think having the students order the objects in terms of disc-ness really helps them get to the concept of ratio more easily."

At the end of Workshop 3, the teachers reflect on the ways in which the PSC process has helped them grow professionally. Kaitlin's teachers share that this cycle has provided them with a better understanding of the applications of ratios, increased knowledge about how middle school students develop proportional thinking, and an expanded repertoire of teaching strategies to move their own students forward developmentally.

INSIGHTS FROM THE DISC PROBLEM VIGNETTES

Like the teachers who participated in Kaitlyn's Disc Problem workshops, teachers who take part in the PSC generally report that the learning they experience in a given cycle goes far beyond the specific problem used in those three workshops. Naturally, they develop a deeper understanding of the mathematical concepts and skills central to the PSC problem, but even more important, they learn the power of deeply investigating a shared mathematical and pedagogical experience. Of course, it is not feasible for mathematics teachers to analyze each problem they use in the classroom at the same level of detail as they do with the PSC problems. Nor is that the intent of this PD model. However, teachers who participated in multiple iterations of the PSC have told us that as a result of those ongoing experiences they think very differently about mathematics instruction and have made strides toward increasing their students' learning opportunities. As Jordan told our iPSC research team:

> I think the Problem-Solving Cycle really helps teachers take a good look at themselves and a good look at student thinking. It helps us become better at analyzing student thinking so that we know how to teach toward that thinking. Once we can figure out how the students are thinking, then the sky's the limit for the learning that's going to take place in that classroom.

Another participant, Shana, reflected:

> I've learned from the PSC to be a much more reflective teacher. I've learned not to guide my students directly to one particular answer, but to let them have time to think and come up with answers in different ways because there's always more than one way to do something. The PSC model helps teachers learn how to constantly improve their teaching, not to think that we've arrived because no teacher ever arrives but to continually strive to get better and try hard to push our students forward in their mathematical thinking.

CHAPTER 4

The Role of Video in the PSC

> I think that watching and discussing video clips was the single most valuable part of the STAAR program. I have learned the most about my teaching by watching my teaching practice. Even better, though, was watching others teach a lesson that I also taught. My ideas have been sparked by others in this group. Having a safe place to watch ourselves and not feel like we were being criticized or evaluated was critical also.
>
> —Ken's written reflection at the end of the STAAR project

As developers of the PSC, we are often asked: Is video really a critical component of the PSC? Can I leave it out and still do the PSC? We respond that video truly is a central component of the PSC model. Although it is certainly possible to lead effective professional development without video, it is not possible to effectively carry out the PSC without video. In this chapter, we explore the rationale behind the use of video in the PSC. We also describe how we have used video, the importance of a supportive community, and the flexibility built into the PSC where video is concerned. Finally, we share our research findings about how teachers' conversations and interactions around video can develop over time.

WHY USE VIDEO IN PD?

Video is central to the PSC as a means of encouraging reflection and insight into teaching and learning. Video has the unique capability of capturing the complexity of classroom instruction in a way that can be studied, analyzed, and shared. Watching and reflecting on video helps highlight aspects of teachers' lessons that they may not notice when they are in the midst of teaching. It also provides other teachers with a window into their colleagues' lessons and supports the community in recognizing how much they stand to learn from one another and from their students.

The Value of Viewing Teaching Snapshots

In the PSC, teachers generally see only small portions of one another's lessons. Viewing short clips allows the group to focus on specific moments in a lesson, in order to make sense of precisely what is happening and engage in meaningful conversations tied to selected instances of learning and instruction. Video slows down the typically fast-paced dynamics of classroom life. Teachers can pause, rewind, and replay an interesting, confusing, or surprising interaction.

When teachers watch a video clip together as a group, they bring multiple perspectives to the table—especially with respect to how they interpret the content, student reasoning, and instructional strategies. The PSC encourages collaborative engagement that is focused on reflection, analysis, and the consideration of alternative teaching strategies, all based on concrete images of classroom lessons. In the PSC, the primary purpose of watching and analyzing video is to make teaching episodes transparent and open for exploration. Discussions are not meant to spur evaluations or critiques of specific teachers. Rather, PSC workshops are intended to be forums for inquiry into teaching and learning, and to help generate ideas that are relevant and of interest to the participants.

One early participant in the iPSC project, Robert, sent an email to the other mathematics teachers in his district encouraging them to join the study. Having worked with video in previous professional development programs and knowing that some teachers might be daunted by the use of videos, Robert wrote:

> The value of the videos does not lie in the determination of right and wrong practices, particularly in a given situation. It lies in the ability to stop the flight of time and have a rich discussion on what happened, how, why, and what else might have been possible at that time. Teachers do not learn how to correct given situations, but how to absorb more of what is happening in a classroom and how to have more options to choose from on the fly. They become more aware of the classroom situation, and thus become more effective at responding to events as they happen.

The Importance of Using Video from Participants' Own Classrooms

Incorporating video from any teacher's classroom situates the professional development in a setting that is likely to prove meaningful. However, several researchers report that teachers find watching video from their own classrooms or the classrooms of colleagues to be more motivating and to support their learning better than video from unfamiliar teachers' classrooms (Seidel,

Stürmer, Blomberg, Kobarg, & Schwindt, 2011; Zhang, Lundeberg, Koehler, & Eberhardt, 2011). Video makes teachers' own classrooms accessible in a way that other media simply cannot, and therefore it has the potential to be a powerful catalyst for change and improvement (LeFevre, 2004).

Using video from *participants' own* classrooms is a central tenet of the PSC model. As we described previously, each iteration of the PSC begins by having teachers collaboratively solve and discuss a designated mathematical problem. Next, they modify the problem according to the needs of their own classroom context and then use it with their students. When teachers' lessons are videotaped, clips from those lessons provide a natural springboard for conversations about student reasoning and instructional strategies that are highly relevant for the entire group. By watching the clips, participants see themselves and their colleagues working in a known context, using a highly familiar problem. All of these elements combine to provide teachers with a unique opportunity to deeply investigate mathematics teaching and learning, consider effective instructional practices, and generate ideas about how to better meet the needs of their student population.

In our experience, teachers who participate in the PSC overwhelmingly find watching and analyzing video from their own lessons and their colleagues' lessons to be a positive experience. For many, viewing and discussing video is the most valuable aspect of the professional development. Observing themselves and their colleagues in action helps teachers better appreciate their students' capacity for mathematical reasoning, learn new pedagogical strategies, and define common challenges. In addition, viewing footage from their own classrooms allows teachers to contemplate what they are doing well and identify areas for improvement. Teachers engage in discussions about topics that are important and relevant to them, and they become increasingly motivated to improve their teaching skills and better serve their students. As another participant in the iPSC project, Hannah, reflected,

> I learned so much about my students and classroom from watching the video. When I watched my video, I was shocked and amazed about how many conversations were happening in my classroom. Watching the video has made me reflect and change my instructional practices.

HOW TO USE VIDEO IN PSC WORKSHOPS

Integral to the PSC model is that fact that each workshop follows a general outline and features a specific goal (or goals) as determined by the facilitator. In PSC Workshop 1, for example, facilitators select the PSC problem and teacher-analysis task based on their objectives for supporting the teaching and learning of specific mathematical content. The manner in which facilitators guide teachers to discuss the teacher-analysis task—especially the probing questions they ask during group discussions—helps highlight their intentions and ensure that the group stays on track.

In the same way, facilitators set goals related to their selection and use of video during PSC Workshops 2 and 3. To generate these goals, facilitators can ask themselves questions such as:

- What do I notice when I watch the teachers' lessons?
- What video clips would help the teachers explore particular issues without causing stifling discomfort for the group members or disempowering them as professionals?
- In what ways could the clips help teachers better understand the mathematical content and practices in the Common Core State Standards?
- What questions would help focus the teachers' attention and stimulate conversations?
- How should multiple clips be sequenced to best provide opportunities for learning?

Selecting Video Clips

As noted in Chapter 2, selecting relatively short, manageable clips from actual mathematics lessons is a challenging but critical component of facilitating the PSC. Because the video clips originate from PSC lessons taught by the participating teachers, the choice of clips is limited by the number of lessons that were videotaped and the quality of those video recordings. Thus, what the teachers did in their lessons and the ways the lessons unfolded set the parameters for the topics that are available for exploration. At the same time, in the PSC, video clips are expected to help launch conversations about issues relevant to teaching and learning, not to serve as models of "expert instruction." We have found that when PSC facilitators keep this purpose in mind, they do not have trouble finding appropriate video clips to use in their workshops.

Facilitating Video-Based Discussions During PSC Workshops

Although the conversations generated by video clips are framed by the facilitator's goals and guiding questions, they naturally have some degree of open-endedness. To provide a sense of what these conversations may look like, we draw from a workshop of a facilitator, Mandy, who used the Lemonade Problem (adapted from Van de Walle, 2007, as shown in Figure 4.1) in the first PSC iteration she facilitated during the iPSC project. The Lemonade Problem involves a comparison of two containers of lemonade, and solvers must determine which one has a stronger lemon flavor.

Figure 4.1. The Lemonade Problem

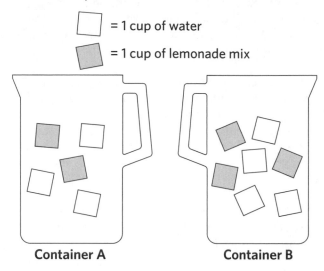

Here are two recipes to make lemonade. The containers are full.

☐ = 1 cup of water

▨ = 1 cup of lemonade mix

Container A   **Container B**

Mandy's workshop included three other mathematics teachers from her school: Nicole, Ellie, and James. After watching the videos of her teachers' lessons using the Lemonade Problem and talking informally with them about how the lessons went, Mandy decided her Workshop 3 should focus on helping students consider two variables simultaneously when they are solving a mixture problem. In particular, she wanted the teachers to consider how to assist students who used additive rather than multiplicative reasoning. With that goal in mind, she selected two clips from Nicole's lesson to show the group.

Mandy tells the group that they will watch two video clips from Nicole's Lemonade Problem lesson that show how a student, Janelle, solved the problem. Their objective, initially, is to try to understand what Janelle was thinking. In the first clip, Janelle comes to the front of the room to show her solution strategy on the Smart Board (see Figure 4.2). Using the picture provided, Janelle crosses off a cup of water in Container A and a cup of water in Container B. Then she crosses off a cup of lemonade mix in Container A and a cup of lemonade mix in Container B. This process continues until everything in Container A has been crossed off and Container B is left with one cup of water and one cup of lemonade mix.

After watching this clip twice, Mandy's group agrees that although they had anticipated solution strategies where students "pair" cups of water and lemonade mix within containers, they had not anticipated this sort of "elimination" strategy across containers, which they liken to "canceling" in

Figure 4.2. Janelle's Solution

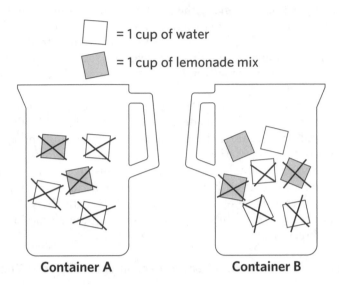

= 1 cup of water

= 1 cup of lemonade mix

Container A   **Container B**

mathematical equations. Nicole relates that she was surprised to see several students in her class using this strategy.

Before watching the second clip, in which Janelle completes her answer to the problem, the group predicts that she will say that Container B has a stronger lemonade flavor, or possibly that the lemonade flavor in the containers is the same. In fact, in the second clip Janelle says that she thinks Container A will have the stronger flavor, but she does not clearly explain why. The teachers laugh with surprise and exclaim, "How did she pick A?" Mandy encourages them to take up this question, but they are highly uncertain about what Janelle might be thinking.

Mandy decides to shift the conversation toward a consideration of instructional strategies. She asks, "Based on what we know, what are Nicole's options to support student learning, to move students in a direction where they can develop an understanding of ratio?" The teachers respond that students who have little background with ratios, such as Janelle, require support in looking at two variables at once. They agree that it may be beneficial for students to try out various incorrect approaches—such as eliminating, canceling, and subtracting—in order to understand why proportional reasoning is appropriate in these situations. Mandy tells the group that later on in the lesson, Janelle argues that Container A has a stronger flavor because it contains less water. The teachers mull this reasoning over. They agree that Janelle is most likely only considering the amount of water in each container, and has concluded that less water yields a stronger lemonade flavor regardless of the amount of lemonade mix.

The two short video clips that Mandy selected, in which a student grapples with the Lemonade Problem using an erroneous "elimination" strategy, afford a lively discussion among the teachers in her group. Mandy thought hard about both the video clips and her guiding questions, and she was pleased with the result. She reflected, "I was prepared with different types of questions and things to ask them to keep the focus moving in the right direction. Working off that lesson, I wanted to connect it to our daily teaching practice."

As this vignette illustrates, selecting engaging video clips is not enough; effective use of video in the PSC depends on well-prepared facilitators who create learning opportunities through purposeful planning and specific objectives to guide group activities and discussions. Successful facilitators, much like improvisational actors and musicians, work in the moment, adapting their questions to build on teachers' reactions and highlight salient ideas. Careful planning and deep familiarity with the video clips enable them to recognize opportunities to ensure that the discussion moves in productive directions.

Encouraging Teachers to Watch and Reflect on Their Videos by Themselves

In addition to watching video clips as a group during PSC workshops, it is important for teachers to have the opportunity to view and reflect individually on their own videotaped lessons, usually prior to PSC Workshop 2. Therefore, we always make sure that teachers have a copy of their full lesson. This enables them to watch the video in the privacy of their own homes and attend to whatever issues strike them, such as their use of particular pedagogical strategies or their students' thinking about particular topics.

Although some teachers are eager to see their lessons on video, others may need prodding in order to watch them. Facilitators can take various steps to encourage teachers to view their lessons—for example, by having them select clips to share during the PD (with the full group or just with partners), or by asking them to write down some reflections (such as insights about students' reasoning or aspects of the lesson that surprised them). Once teachers become comfortable watching their own videos, they typically report that they can critically notice and interpret classroom interactions that they missed while working in "real time."

THE IMPORTANCE OF A SUPPORTIVE COMMUNITY

The development of teacher learning communities is difficult and time-consuming work, yet it is work with a large payoff. Establishing and maintaining a safe and professional community is especially important when teachers are asked to share video clips with their colleagues. Watching and discussing video is likely to seem more threatening to teachers than sharing other artifacts such as student work and lesson plans. To be willing to take such a risk, teachers must feel confident that showing their videos will provide learning opportunities for both themselves and their colleagues, and that the atmosphere will be one of productive discourse—without value judgments regarding either the teacher or the students.

In a carefully structured PD setting, analyzing video can help foster a tight-knit and supportive community. To create and sustain this type of community, teachers must communicate openly yet respectfully, and they must agree upon appropriate discourse norms to support such communication. Because viewing video of themselves and their colleagues may be a new experience for teachers, we encourage PSC facilitators to explicitly share how they expect conversations around video to unfold, beginning with the first time they use video in their PSC workshops and reminding teachers of these expectations as often as necessary. It is the facilitator's job to be sure teachers remember that in the PSC, the purpose of watching and discussing video is not to evaluate or criticize, but to investigate student thinking and to explore the potential implications of various teaching practices. One set of norms generated by a group of PSC facilitators in preparation for conducting their first Workshop 2 is shown in Figure 4.3.

Because teachers' actions and voices are a core component of PSC workshops, the participants should feel included and empowered to assume ownership of their learning. In our experience, as teachers work together to study

Figure 4.3. Norms for Watching Video Developed by a Group of PSC Facilitators

Norms for Watching Video

- Video clips are examples, not exemplars.
  - To spur discussion not criticism

- Video clips are for investigation of teaching and learning, not evaluation of the teacher.
  - To spur inquiry not judgment

- Video clips are snapshots of teaching, not an entire lesson.
  - To focus attention on a particular moment, not what came before or after

- Video clips are for examination of a particular interaction.
  - To provide evidence for claims by citing specific examples

and improve their practice, the community grows stronger, and the group becomes more comfortable with and adept at collaboratively exploring what they see on the video. Facilitators can capitalize on advances in the teachers' analytical skills and the increasing strength of their professional learning community to help them delve into more complex mathematical content and instances of teaching and learning that content. Our data show that PSC facilitators are generally quite successful in this regard. That is, the PSC facilitators we have studied carefully attended to the development of a community in which there is respect, trust, and collegial working relationships. Such a climate leads to willingness on the teachers' part to expose their instructional practices and to engage in increasingly reflective and productive conversations around video, which in turn supports professional growth and improvement.

FLEXIBILITY IN THE USE OF VIDEO AS PART OF THE PSC

The use of video as a central component of professional development may at first seem daunting to facilitators and nerve-wracking to teachers. However, there is a large degree of flexibility built into the PSC with regard to how video is introduced and used in workshops. The facilitators we studied employed a wide variety of strategies to help teachers become more comfortable with the use of video in the PSC, including initially showing clips from the facilitators' own classrooms and modeling what it is like to be the object of discussion. In addition, prior to using a clip selected from a participant's PSC lesson, facilitators have found it beneficial to check with the participant, both to make sure he or she is willing to have that particular clip shown and so the participant is not caught off-guard. Another strategy we have found to be effective is to use clips that largely (or entirely) show students, such as their evolving work on a problem or their conversations in small groups. Even teachers who are initially reluctant to have their lessons recorded may be persuaded to have a camera in the room that enables them to see what their students are doing when they are working in groups. As the vignette with the Lemonade Problem illustrated, video clips of students can be analyzed from both a "student thinking" perspective (How are these students thinking about the problem at hand?) and a "teacher's role" perspective (What might a teacher do next given what we see in the video?).

When it comes to showing video that includes the participating teachers, facilitators may initially decide to select clips that highlight instructional choices in a fundamentally positive light. As the community bond grows stronger, facilitators can branch out and show clips that capture potentially problematic moments in a classroom, or more mathematically and pedagogically challenging content. In general, facilitators must have their pulse firmly on the group's comfort level around video, and must carefully consider which strategies they can use to decrease any anxiety that might arise.

They walk a fine line between remaining aware of and sensitive to teachers' concerns, and encouraging teachers to grapple with demanding mathematical and pedagogical topics. PSC facilitators should keep this balance in mind when selecting video clips and structuring the workshop environment, to ensure that video is used in a manner that teachers will find valuable, engaging, and productive.

WHAT DOES THE RESEARCH SHOW?

As we implemented the PSC through our grant projects, we were able to collect a wide variety of data on various aspects of the model. One thing we were interested in understanding was how teachers' conversations and interactions around video during the PSC workshops developed and changed over time. In one study during the STAAR project, we recorded a set of PSC workshops that our team facilitated over 2 years and analyzed all the conversations that took place when teachers watched video clips together. Our main research questions were:

1. What was the nature of full-group discussions around video?
2. How did those discussions change over time?

We addressed these questions by looking closely at the three main topics that PSC workshops cover: mathematical content, student thinking, and the teacher's role.

Conversations Around Mathematical Content

From the beginning of their involvement in the STAAR project, the group of teachers we studied engaged in constructive examinations of the mathematical ideas represented in the video clips they watched. We found that over time, these teachers became more comfortable discussing their difficulties with the mathematical content, and not surprisingly, their later conversations were notably more productive than the conversations they had at the beginning. By the end of 2 years, the teachers talked in a more focused, in-depth, and analytical manner about specific issues related to various representations and strategies that could be used to solve the selected PSC problems. In particular, they appeared to feel more comfortable addressing deficits in their knowledge of the mathematical content, without continually making reference to their students or otherwise couching the conversation. Such discussions would likely not have occurred unless all of the necessary elements were in place: specifically, a tight-knit professional community of teachers who were eager to learn, a common mathematical and pedagogical experience, and the use of video to situate the teachers' conversation in a personally relevant context.

Conversations Around Student Thinking

When analyzing video clips of students solving a PSC problem or explaining their ideas, the teachers in our study initially attended to what the students were doing and saying, the mathematical validity of student-generated solution methods, and evidence that individual students were learning. By the end of the study, the teachers more often engaged in conversations in which they analyzed the students' reasoning. Their conversations were considerably longer, produced more nuanced insights into students' mathematical ideas, and more clearly advanced the teachers' own conceptual understanding of the problems.

As an example, in one of the final workshops of the STAAR project, the teachers watched a clip of a small group of students working on a PSC problem. The clip showed one student, Leo, explaining his solution method and reasoning to his peers. The facilitators of this workshop selected the clip because Leo's method was one that had not been used by any of the teachers when they solved the problem themselves during Workshop 1, nor had the teachers anticipated this method when they planned their PSC lessons. After watching the clip together, the teachers talked at length about Leo's strategy, not only to verify that it was accurate but also to consider how his emerging idea could be developed into a generalizable formula. The teachers engaged in some of the calculations they imagined Leo and his fellow students might have employed, using the video clip as the impetus to investigate important algebraic concepts much more deeply than they had done previously.

The PSC participants' expanding analytical skills and eagerness to engage in conversations about challenging mathematical topics prompted them to better appreciate their students' unique and often sophisticated approaches to problems, and to reflect on implications for their planning and teaching. Rather than getting tired of continued examinations of the same problem, the teachers gained new understandings that they planned to take back to their classrooms. There was general agreement among the group that these understandings would assist them in future decisionmaking processes, including how to better prepare their students for this problem or similar ones, how to plan lessons based on similar content, and how to capitalize on their students' developing ideas. As one STAAR participant, Ken, reflected after the discussion:

> I will be able to help kids more because I now understand these two ways to solve the problem. I understand how one connects to the other. So I will probably be able to ask better questions.

Another participant, Laura, added:

Today was the first day that really solidified my understanding of this problem. . . . I think that knowledge will help me understand where the kids are going the next time I teach it, and understand their thinking a little bit better.

Conversations Around the Teacher's Role

When the teachers in the STAAR project first discussed video clips from their PSC lessons through the lens of the teacher's role, they appeared cautious and hesitant to explore pedagogical issues in great depth. For example, the group spent much of the workshop time describing events that took place in their classrooms and comparing them to the events shown in the video clips. One possible explanation for this is that many teachers felt their first lesson using a PSC problem did not go as well as they had hoped and were disappointed by what they saw when they watched their own videos. Therefore, they used the time to decompress and share stories. When asked to ponder the merits of the videotaped teacher's approach to introducing the problem, the group instead focused on concerns related to their own students. Turning the spotlight onto the students and providing empathy in this regard may have helped the group further establish a supportive and protective community, while sidestepping a more critical discussion of pedagogical strategies. As they continued to work together, the teachers became considerably more comfortable discussing the pros and cons of different approaches to teaching the PSC problems and analyzing the impact of those approaches on student learning. The teachers also reported gaining powerful insights about aspects of their teaching that they felt could be improved.

For example, near the end of the study, the teachers analyzed a video clip in which a teacher, Peter, was talking with a student, Cara, about her method of solving the PSC problem. The facilitators selected the clip because it provided an opportunity to explore the central theme of the workshop: teacher questioning. Toward the conclusion of the discussion, Peter suggested to the group that his interactions with Cara appeared to have limited, rather than expanded, her thinking about the mathematics in the problem. He commented that rather than trying to understand and encourage her mathematical reasoning, "I was trying to force her toward my solution." When asked what he wished he had done differently, Peter answered, "I wish I had stopped talking for about 5 seconds and looked at her solution." He noted that a more productive alternative might have been to ask the other students in his class to consider how Cara came up with her expression. The facilitators and other teachers agreed that using a student's method as the focal point for a whole-class discussion can be a powerful instructional move. Several also acknowledged that they have been in Peter's shoes and have simply steered their own students down the desired path.

In an interview at the end of the project, Peter reflected that he has become increasingly "hands-off" and more attentive to building on his students' thinking. Peter explained that watching his own video helped him notice that he was "forcing students toward a conclusion," and he now "actively monitors" himself to make sure he uses different strategies.

RESEARCH CONCLUSIONS

Our data from the STAAR project show that when teachers watch and discuss video as part of the PSC, they can develop an expanded willingness and ability to inquire into important issues related to mathematics teaching and learning. In addition, the teachers we studied responded positively to progressively more challenging prompts from the facilitators, leading to more in-depth and meaningful conversations. At the same time, the facilitators were successful at maintaining a supportive environment in which the participants showed concern and respect for the teachers and students shown in the video clips. These results support the premise that using teachers' own video to ground conversations in the PSC can be a powerful tool for promoting reflection and growth. In the next chapter, we take a different look at how the PSC can impact participating teachers' knowledge and instructional practices, and their students' mathematics achievement.

Impact of the PSC on Teacher Knowledge and Instruction and on Student Achievement

What evidence is there that the PSC can impact the participants' mathematical knowledge, their instructional practices, and the mathematics achievement of their students? In this chapter, we present findings from analyses we have conducted looking at the PSC's impact in each of these areas. Overall, it seems clear that the PSC offers teachers and their students the potential for significant growth. Although individual results may vary, on the whole our data show that the PSC model supports improvements within a relatively short time frame.

We begin by looking at changes in teachers' knowledge for a group of PSC participants. Then we move to an examination of the impact of the PSC on teachers' instructional practice. Here, we present quantitative data along with an illustrative case study of one participant, Ken. Finally, we explore the impact of the PSC on student achievement by comparing mathematics achievement data for three groups of students: students of participating teachers in one district, students of nonparticipating teachers in the same district, and students across the state. The various analyses are based on different combinations of data from the original STAAR project and the 4 years of data in the iPSC project. For each analysis, we identify the specific sets of participants it includes.

IMPACT ON TEACHER KNOWLEDGE

As mentioned in Chapter 1, a primary goal of the PSC is to provide teachers with opportunities to expand their mathematical knowledge for teaching. In order to gauge whether participation in the iPSC actually impacted the teachers' MKT, we asked the teachers who took part in Year 1, 2, and/or 3 to complete pre- and post-administrations of the Mathematical Knowledge for Teaching (MKT) assessment. Deborah Ball and colleagues developed the MKT assessment as a means of gathering information about teachers' mathematical content knowledge and their pedagogical content knowledge. The MKT assessment tests this type of knowledge by requiring teachers to make judgments similar to those they make during classroom instruction (Ball, Hill, & Bass, 2005; Hill, Sleep, Lewis, & Ball, 2007). For example, a teacher may be asked to explain a mathematical rule, consider the accuracy of an unusual solution method, or decide which of several definitions is most appropriate for students at a particular grade level.

We used a version of the MKT assessment that is specifically geared for middle school (consistent with the fact that we worked with middle school teachers) and focused on number concepts and operations (consistent with the fact that we emphasized ratio and proportion with those teachers). We gave the teachers two parallel forms of the MKT assessment[1]; they completed one form before they took part in their first PSC workshop, and they completed the other form at the end of their participation in our research project (that is, after 1 or 2 academic years, depending on the teacher). (See Figure 5.1 for an example of a sample item from the middle school MKT assessment related to ratio.)

Figure 5.1. Sample MKT Middle School Item

Mr. Garrison's students were comparing different rectangles and decided to find the ratio of height to width. They wondered, though, if it would matter whether they measured the rectangles using inches or using centimeters.

As the class discussed the issue, Mr. Garrison decided to give them other examples to consider. For each situation below, decide whether it is an example for which different ways of measuring produce the same ratio or a different ratio. For each situation, check one of the following: (1) produces same ratio, (2) produces different ratio, or (3) I'm not sure.

	Produces Same Ratio	Produces Different Ratio	I'm Not Sure
a. The ratio of two people's heights measured in (1) feet or (2) meters.			
b. The noontime temperatures yesterday and today, measured in (1) Fahrenheit or (2) Centigrade.			
c. The speeds of two airplanes, measured in (1) feet per second or (2) miles per hour.			
d. The growths of two bank accounts, measured in (1) annual percentage increase or (2) end-of-year balance minus beginning-of-year balance.			

On average, the 62 teachers who completed both MKT assessments showed significant knowledge gains. On the pretest, the teachers answered an average of 66.5% of the problems correctly, whereas on the posttest, they answered an average of 71.9% of the problems correctly, a gain of 5.4%. It is important to note that we did not gather similar data from a control sample of teachers; therefore, it is possible that the knowledge increases we observed might have occurred regardless of the teachers' participation in the PSC—for example, because of other professional development experiences in which they might have engaged during the time of the project.

CHANGES IN INSTRUCTIONAL PRACTICES

We view teacher professional development as a career-long endeavor, and likewise we see the improvement of classroom instruction as a long-term undertaking. In the following sections, we explore instructional changes that were evident over the course of the teachers' participation in the PSC. First, we present quantitative data analyses based on a set of videotaped lessons that highlight the nature of participants' PSC and "typical" (i.e., non-PSC) lessons and how they changed over time. Then, we present a case study to document the evolving nature of one teacher's lessons during the course of his participation in the PSC. Within the case study analyses, we explore two facets of his instructional transformation: supporting small-group work and promoting students' mathematical thinking.

Quantitative Patterns of Instructional Change

In both the STAAR and the iPSC projects, our research team was motivated by the vision of school mathematics portrayed in the National Council of Teachers of Mathematics' (NCTM, 2000) *Principles and Standards for School Mathematics*. In our meetings with teachers and/or teacher leaders, we emphasized the importance of engaging students in activities such as exploring, justifying, proving, critiquing, and generalizing important mathematical ideas. In order to determine the impact of the PSC on the participants' classroom instruction, we looked at the extent to which these types of practices were incorporated, over time, in their mathematics lessons. To this end, we collected video recordings of participating teachers' PSC and typical lessons throughout both projects. One set of analyses focused on mathematics lessons taught by the 13 teachers who participated in the initial 2 years of the PSC project. During the first year, we videotaped five teacher leaders, and in the second year we videotaped the same five teacher leaders along with eight teachers who attended their PSC workshops. Each semester we recorded two of their lessons: one PSC lesson and one typical lesson. Here, we present analyses based on the teachers' first and last videotaped PSC and typical lessons, totaling 51 lessons.

We analyzed these lessons using an instrument called the Mathematical Quality of Instruction (MQI) observation scale, also developed by Deborah Ball and her colleagues (Learning Mathematics for Teaching Project, 2011). The MQI is derived from and aligned with the NCTM Standards (NCTM, 2000), and it provides a framework to analyze teachers' classroom instructional practices (Kilday & Kinzie, 2009). The instrument measures four dimensions of instruction:[2] (1) richness of the mathematics, (2) working with students and mathematics, (3) errors and imprecision, and (4) student participation in meaning-making and reasoning. Within each of these dimensions, we rated a set of three to six items on a 3-point scale (low, mid-, or high) for each 7.5-minute lesson segment. Table 5.1 provides a descriptive example of what a high rating would look like within each dimension. In addition, there are two items that describe the overall lesson in terms of the mathematical quality of instruction and the teacher's estimated mathematical knowledge for teaching. For these two items, we used a 5-point rating scale (poor, fair, good, very good, or excellent).

Dimension averages. As Figure 5.2 shows, overall, teachers made the largest improvements in the *working with students and mathematics* dimension, for both their PSC and typical lessons. This finding suggests that over time, the teachers were better able to understand and build on their students' mathematical ideas and help them work through their errors in a conceptual manner. Teachers' PSC lessons increased slightly in the *richness of mathematics* dimension (while remaining constant for the typical lessons), indicating that the teachers included more opportunities for students to engage in rich mathematics in their later PSC lessons—for example, by encouraging mathematical explanations or identifying multiple ways of solving problems. The *errors and imprecision* dimension decreased slightly for the typical lessons, while remaining constant for the PSC lessons. The rate at which teachers made errors when presenting mathematical content in their typical lessons fell to approximately the level of their PSC lessons. The *student participation* dimension decreased somewhat for both the PSC and typical lessons, suggesting that the teachers were less focused on ensuring that their students contributed to meaning-making in the classroom. (We did not run tests of statistical significance on the MQI data because of the small sample size.)

Looking at these patterns another way, one might notice that *student participation* is actually the dimension that was consistently rated the highest across the lessons and time periods. Although the ratings did drop, it is possible that teachers were increasingly focused on ensuring that their lessons contained sufficient mathematical richness and conceptual work for students, and they focused somewhat less on ensuring the same high levels of student participation.

Table 5.1. Mathematical Quality of Instruction (MQI) Rating Categories and Examples

Rating Categories	Scale	Example/Explanation of High Rating
Mathematical richness	1–3	A teacher engages her students in a discussion about what cylindrical means, asking them for definitions, examples, and counterexamples. She has a variety of objects for them to reference, draws accurate diagrams as references, and promotes the use of mathematical language such as *lateral area.*
Working with students	1–3	Students are working in small groups on a challenging problem. The teacher walks around and carefully listens to each group. He then talks to the students at length about their ideas, based on their current conceptions. The teacher asks questions to either help the students recognize their own misunderstandings or to extend their thinking.
Errors and imprecision	1–3	A teacher works with her students to interpret a table about the percentage of the population in various countries that have telephones. The teacher makes a number of inaccurate statements such as "Less than 1% of the people in Chad decided they needed a telephone. And yet, more than 100% of the people in the United States decided they needed a telephone." *This portion of the lesson was coded "high" for errors and imprecision.*
Student participation	1–3	Toward the end of a class period, students present posters they have created that show their various solutions to a complex problem. The students explain their ideas and answer challenging questions from the teacher and other students.
Overall MQI	1–5	A teacher spends the full class period having his students work on a rich task, ensuring that they are deeply engaged, providing remediation that is conceptual in nature, encouraging the students to generalize their ideas when appropriate, and so on.
Overall MKT	1–5	A teacher consistently demonstrates a high degree of knowledge about the content covered in the lesson and effectively helps her students make sense of the content.

Figure 5.2. Dimension Averages for PSC and Typical Lessons

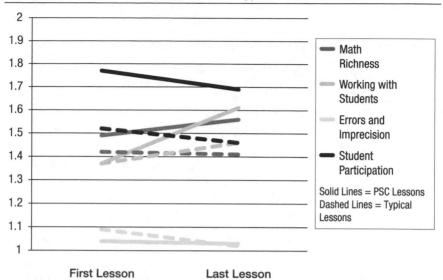

Working with students and mathematics. We now take a closer look at the dimension that showed the greatest improvement, *working with students.* There are three items on the MQI within this dimension: (1) conceptual remediation of student errors and difficulties, (2) responding to students' mathematical productions, and (3) overall working with students and mathematics. Table 5.2 provides examples of teacher–student interactions that would be coded as "high" for each of these three items. As Figure 5.3 shows, ratings on all three items increased to some extent over time, for both the PSC and typical lessons. Similar to the patterns in the dimension averages (Figure 5.2), teachers' PSC lessons were almost always rated higher than their typical lessons. Teachers generally received the highest ratings for responding to students, indicating that their students made substantive mathematical contributions and the teacher responded to those contributions in mathematically appropriate ways. Although the teachers' ratings for conceptual remediation were a bit lower than their ratings for responding to students, the teachers were making strides in improving this aspect of their instruction.

Overall mathematical quality of instruction. As previously noted, the MQI instrument includes an overall rating of each lesson's mathematical quality of instruction. Highly rated lessons include elements such as productive teacher–student interactions around the math content, few teacher errors, and a sharp mathematical focus that enables students to develop the important ideas under consideration. Figure 5.4 displays the percentage of

Table 5.2. Examples of High Ratings on Items in the Working with Students Category

Rating Categories	Definition of High Rating	Example of High Rating
Remediation of student errors	Teacher engages in conceptual remediation systematically and at length.	Students are asked to come up with a method for determining the relative steepness of various ramps. One group of students decides to measure steepness by multiplying a ramp's length and height. Without indicating whether this strategy is correct, the teacher asks the students to explain what bigger or smaller products mean in this context. The students say that ramps with smaller products have smaller slopes. The teacher tells them to test their idea on more objects, and when they do so, the students recognize that their strategy is inaccurate.
Responding to students	Teacher identifies important student insights and builds instruction based on students' ideas.	A student suggests that steepness can be found by multiplying a ramp's length and height, and then dividing by two. Others in the group recognize this strategy as finding the area. The teacher asks whether area is the same as steepness and fosters a rich discussion that leads the students to conclude that the two things are different. In doing so, different ideas emerge for the group to explore.
Overall work with students	Teacher understands and uses students' ideas and errors in an outstanding way.	A group of students is calculating steepness by subtracting the height from the length of each ramp. The teacher encourages the students to graph their results and visually inspect whether their graph matches their expectations.

Figure 5.3. Working with Students Categories for PSC and Typical Lessons

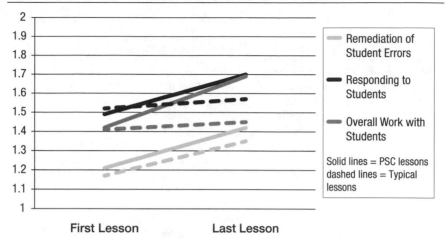

teachers' lessons that were rated as poor, fair, good, very good, and excellent. All of the PSC lessons were judged to be either "good" or "very good," with a pronounced increase in "very good" ratings over time. There was a wider range in the ratings of the typical lessons. The teachers' early typical lessons ranged from "poor" to "excellent." Their later typical lessons ranged from "fair" to "very good," with notably more "good" and "very good" lessons. In general, the PSC lessons were rated higher on overall quality of instruction relative to the typical lessons.

Illustrative Case Study: Ken's Instructional Change

We turn now to an exploration of Ken's classroom teaching, and how his instruction changed over the 2-year period that he was part of the STAAR project. We selected Ken in order to provide a detailed example of the experiences and classroom practices of one teacher who participated in the PSC. We do not claim that our case study of Ken is representative of the experience of all the teachers in the STAAR project; however, a careful examination of his instructional growth demonstrates the PSC's potential for supporting change. We recorded 14 of Ken's lessons over this time period, interviewed him after each videotaped lesson, and collected his written reflections after each PSC workshop. In addition to analyzing the nature of the changes in Ken's instruction, we also considered Ken's interpretations of these changes and his goals with respect to improving his instruction.

Throughout the project, Ken maintained a consistent and outspoken desire to learn and was deeply committed to improving his understanding of mathematical content and his mathematics instruction. Shortly after the

Figure 5.4. Overall MQI Ratings By Category for PSC and Typical Lessons

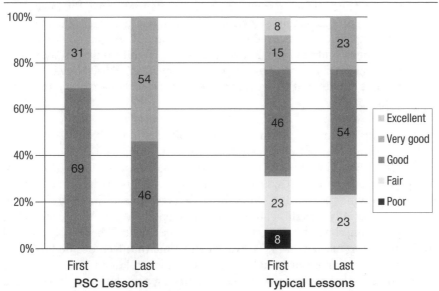

conclusion of the project, Ken won a "teacher of the year" award presented by his district. The fact that our research group had no part in nominating or judging teachers for this award suggests that Ken's efforts to improve were noticed and respected by his colleagues in his school and across the district.

Ken's background. Ken had taught 5th- and 6th-grade mathematics for 3 years when he joined the STAAR project. He taught 6th-grade math for both years of the study. Ken worked in a K–8 school in a medium-sized, suburban school district. Minority students comprised approximately half of the district's population, and over a quarter of the students were eligible for free or reduced-price lunch. The percentages of minority students and students eligible for free or reduced-price lunch at Ken's school were similar to those in the district. Ken had completed a master's degree in education, and near the end of our program, he began working toward his principal licensure. He is currently working as an assistant principal at an elementary school in the same district.

Supporting small-group work. From the beginning of his participation in the PSC, Ken was strongly affected by the experience of working on mathematical problems in small groups, and he vowed to incorporate more group-work in his own lessons. At the end of the 2-week summer session that kicked off the STAAR project, Ken reflected:

I began to rethink my teaching. I usually keep all the kids in rows separated and all facing front. To me, it seems that I have the fewest discipline problems this way, especially with the kids talking while I am talking. Then it occurred to me that in the PSC workshops we are talking nearly all the time. But we are talking about math! Fascinating! How can I get this kind of atmosphere in my class? Well, I haven't quite figured it out yet, but the goal is there, and it's what I am going to shoot for this fall.

Over the 2-year period in which Ken took part in the PSC, he gradually reduced the amount of time his students spent working as a whole class and increased the amount of time they spent in small groups. Ken's shift from having his students sit in rows to having them sit in clusters happened immediately following the first PSC workshop. Ken recognized that working with their peers initially was difficult for some students: "Working in groups has been something that's been pretty tough because the kids haven't been used to doing that in mathematics." It was at this time that Ken decided to focus on establishing group norms in his classroom. He explained in an interview: "I try to really stress the importance of working together and cooperating with the people who are in your group. And I try to stress that everyone in a group is a resource."

By the end of his participation in the STAAR project, Ken used group-work time in increasingly unique ways to promote in-depth, student-led conversations. For example, in his final videotaped PSC lesson, we observed Ken walking around the room and listening carefully to each group's ideas. At one point he suggested that two of the groups join together to talk about their strategies for deriving a formula for incremental growth. In an interview shortly after the lesson, Ken explained, "The groups were going about the problem in totally different ways, yet they had nearly identical formulas in the end. So this seemed to be a good time to bring the two groups together." In this way, Ken promoted across-group conversations and the processing of multiple strategies during small-group work time.

After 2 years in the PSC, Ken reflected:

I felt like I learned so much, and I was able to make huge gains from just working with people during the PSC workshops and really having a lot of time to solve problems. And it wasn't just sit in a class, listen to a lecture, and get some practice problems for homework, like the way I've been teaching for so long. It really changed my own idea about how to deliver instruction for math. Giving discovery time, instead of just having someone model how to solve the problem. . . . Cooperative grouping, in general, I didn't do it before the PSC. I thought I did, but it was more of a seating arrangement than an approach to teaching. And now, I think it's about letting kids learn from one another in their groups. Kind of backing off from guided instruction and letting them do more discovery in their groups.

Promoting students' mathematical thinking. Promoting mathematical thinking in the classroom, especially by encouraging students to explain and justify their ideas, was a central focus throughout the STAAR project. Ken appeared to internalize this goal over the course of his experience in the PSC, and there are clear differences between his earlier and later lessons with respect to promoting students' mathematical discourse. In Ken's first videotaped lesson, he was attentive to the accuracy of students' answers and not necessarily to the strategies and rationale behind them. The class spent about 15–20 minutes going over the previous day's homework. Students would individually come to the front of the room and write out their solution to a given problem on the chalkboard while Ken and the rest of the students watched in silence. Once the students completed their work, Ken broke the silence by requesting, "Show thumbs up if you agree; thumbs down if you disagree." Looking around the room and observing that most students had their thumbs up, Ken would comment, "All right. Pretty good," and the class would move on to the next problem. Ken then introduced the next assignment, and students worked on it independently for the remainder of the class session.

Ken recognized the inherent lack of student talk that resulted from the way his lessons were structured and carried out. When he was asked to reflect on his teaching during a PSC workshop, Ken wrote, "In my classroom I would like to see more thought-provoking, student-engaging questions and activities that really get kids talking about math." He also wrote, "My teaching goal is to better facilitate student-led discussions." During his participation in the PSC, Ken increasingly prioritized having students work on problems in small groups and then come to the front of the room as a group and share their solution strategies with the whole class. As a final reflection at the end of his participation in the PSC, Ken commented, "I realized the importance of talking about our thinking and giving kids the opportunity to share their ideas."

During a later visit to Ken's class, we videotaped him teaching a lesson using a designated PSC task called the Painted Cubes Problem (see Figure 5.5). Throughout this lesson, Ken moved from group to group and frequently sat down with his students to observe their progress and support their learning. At one point, Ken sat with a group of three students who had just constructed a cube with edges of 4 centimeters in length. He asked them, "How many cubes with one face painted would that be?" After a brief exchange in which one student explained that she calculated 24 cubes (the correct answer) by multiplying 6 times 4, Ken pushed the group to think about a larger cube: "Do you suppose if you have a bigger cube, you are still going to multiply by 6? Is it going to change the way the paint falls on the cube in any way?" The same student who had answered correctly previously responded, "Probably." Ken followed with another question: "How?" The student explained, "Because you're making the cube bigger, so the center cubes are going to increase." Ken continued to probe by asking, "Increase how? How is it going to increase?" The student answered, "More cubes are going to add to the center." Not satisfied that he understood the student's thinking, Ken decided to try a different approach, suggesting, "Why don't you go ahead and build a 5 by 5 by 5 cube. You can add on to that one [the cube the group had been working with]."

As this exchange exemplifies, Ken asked students questions that were aimed at encouraging them to explain and justify their problem-solving strategies, and to ensure that he (and presumably the other students in the group) could follow their thinking. Ken also made an effort to allow his students to move in the direction of their own thinking, rather than asking everyone to think (and solve the problem) in exactly the same way. In an interview conducted near the end of the STAAR project, Ken explained, "It feels so much better to get them to a level of understanding on something that they have ownership of. I mean, those were their ideas. It was so much more valuable to them to be able to go from their own perspective or the way that they thought about it to the end, rather than follow my way of thinking about it."

Figure 5.5. The Painted Cubes Problem

A cube with edges of length 2 centimeters is built from 1-centimeter cubes. If you paint the faces of this cube and then break it into 1-centimeter cubes, how many cubes will be painted on three faces?

- How many will be painted on two faces?
- How many will be painted on one face?
- How many will be unpainted?

What if the length of the edges is different from 2 cm? What if the length of each edge is 3 cm? 50 cm? n cm?

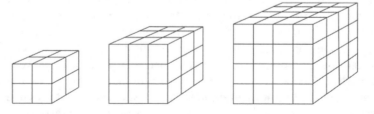

Adapted from Driscoll, 1999, p. 108.

POSITIVE PATTERNS OF CHANGE IN STUDENT ACHIEVEMENT RESULTS

In the iPSC project, our partner school district provided us with student achievement data so that we could gauge the impact of the PSC on student mathematics achievement. Specifically, we looked at the students' Colorado Student Achievement Program (CSAP) mathematics assessment scores. CSAP tests were administered yearly to all Colorado public school students in grades 3 through 10 from 2000 until 2011. For each of the 5 years of the iPSC project (2007–2011), we gathered CSAP mathematics data on the students of middle school teachers who were participating in the PSC during that year, the students of middle school teachers from the same district who were not participating in the PSC that year, and middle school students across the state. Due to frequent changes in the iPSC participant sample, each year of the study we analyzed data only from the students of teachers who were participating that year. (We analyzed spring 2007 data from the students of teachers who began participating in the iPSC in the summer of 2007.)

Figure 5.6 shows, for each category, the percentage of students who scored at a proficient or advanced level on the CSAP. This percentage varied more from year to year for the students of teachers who participated in the

Figure 5.6. Percentage of Students Scoring at the Proficient or Advanced Level on the CSAP

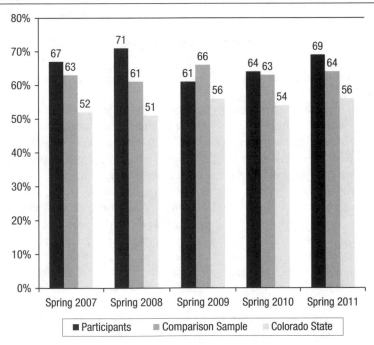

PSC relative to the other groups of students. However, in 4 of the 5 years of the project, the students of the participating teachers earned the highest average CSAP scores. It is also worth noting that this district is relatively high-achieving; in each year of the study, students in the district scored higher than their peers across the state.

When interpreting these data, it is important to keep in mind that the participating schools and teachers in the study changed considerably from year to year. Achievement score variations could be related to the different samples of students who were included in our study each year. Furthermore, neither teachers nor students were randomly assigned, so a variety of factors other than participation in the PSC could account for these findings. At the same time, this portrait of the students' achievement scores over time matches our expectation that the students of participating teachers would exhibit higher test scores than the students of nonparticipating teachers, with the exception of 2009. One possible reason for the dip in the scores of the participants in 2009 is that the sample, for the first time, included "regular teachers" (that is, the teachers who took part in the teacher leaders' PSC workshops) along with teacher leaders. It is plausible that the students of the teacher leaders scored higher on the CSAP relative to the students of the regular teachers, although we did not break the data down in that manner due to the small sample size. It is particularly encouraging that as the participant sample grew (from 2009 to 2011), the students' achievement scores continued to show improvement.

THE PROMISE OF THE PSC

The data presented in this chapter demonstrate the promise of the PSC model of professional development for impacting both teachers and students. We hypothesize that strengthening teachers' mathematical knowledge and fostering gradual change in their classroom instruction are important steps toward increasing the learning opportunities that teachers provide for their students on an everyday basis. The PSC appears to support teachers in making small but critical improvements in their knowledge and practice in ways that promote student learning of mathematics.

At the same time, we realize that teachers are individuals. Even within a group of teachers who participate in the same professional development program, their experiences as learners may vary greatly. Because of teachers' unique circumstances—including the nature of their resources, the school context, their students, and their own identities as teachers—the impact of any given PD, including the PSC, is likely to play out in a variety of ways for the participants.

One especially encouraging finding is the fact that the teachers in our study improved their ability to listen to students' ideas and make sound instructional decisions based on those ideas. Instruction that builds on student thinking is a core feature of the mathematics reform literature (e.g., National Governors Association Center for Best Practices & Council of Chief State School Officers, 2010; NCTM, 2000) and was strongly emphasized in the iPSC project, particularly during the discussions of video from teachers' classrooms in PD workshops. Our analysis of their classroom instruction suggests that both the teacher leaders and the teachers who attended their PSC workshops became increasingly skilled at supporting students' conceptual development of the central mathematical content when teaching PSC lessons. Even more important, these improvements translated to their "typical lessons," which represent the teachers' everyday practice.

NOTES

1. Two forms of a test are considered parallel when they have been developed to be as similar as possible with respect to features such as content, format of the items, and statistical characteristics. One reason to have two forms of a test is to use one as a pretest and another as a posttest.

2. There is also a fifth dimension included in the MQI that examines whether the focus of the classroom work is on mathematics. We coded that dimension but do not report on it here because there were almost no instances in our data set where the classroom work was off topic.

CHAPTER 6

Preparing PSC Facilitators Using the Math Leadership Preparation Model

A key factor in ensuring the effective implementation of any professional development program is having knowledgeable, well-prepared facilitators. Such PD facilitators are typically in high demand, especially as PD efforts ramp up across the United States. At the present time, many individuals who are selected to lead PD are only at the beginning stages of honing their leadership skills. There is a pressing need to prepare these novice PD facilitators so that they become proficient in working with teachers and offering high-quality learning opportunities. However, gaining mastery in the art of facilitation requires focused and extensive preparation.

When we initially designed the PSC as part of the STAAR project, members of our research and development team served as facilitators of the PD workshops. However, the sustainability and scalability of the PSC as a site-based PD model depends on establishing a much larger cadre of qualified local PD leaders. For this reason, we designed a framework for preparing and supporting PSC facilitators called the Mathematics Leadership Preparation (MLP) model. The goal of the MLP is for novice facilitators—typically teachers selected for their leadership capabilities—to develop the understanding and skills needed to plan and lead PSC workshops. Whereas the PSC model helps teachers improve their classroom practice, the MLP model prepares teacher leaders to lead professional development for their colleagues.

We have successfully used this MLP model with several cohorts of mathematics teachers who were interested in leading PSC workshops. Like the PSC, the MLP approach is intended to be flexible, allowing for the unique circumstances and constraints that exist in a given local environment. In this chapter, we describe the MLP model as implemented by our research team during the iPSC project to build the leadership capacity of full-time math teachers who were selected to carry out the PSC at their schools.

THE MLP MODEL

As shown in Figure 6.1, the MLP model includes two main components: (1) a Summer Leadership Academy in which facilitators learn about the

Figure 6.1. Implementing the PSC: Structure of Support for Teacher Leaders

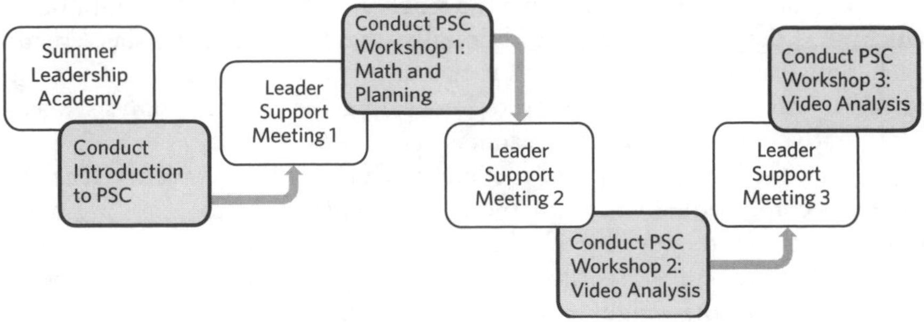

PSC and prepare to lead workshops, and (2) Leader Support Meetings to provide ongoing, structured guidance to the facilitators throughout the academic year. The MLP model incorporates multiple opportunities for participants to learn about and try out PD facilitation practices and receive feedback from both the MLP leaders and their fellow teacher leaders. In addition, the MLP provides a structure within which teacher leaders can consider ways to adapt the PSC to specific needs of the teachers in their schools, while at the same time maintaining the integrity of the goals and design of the PD program.

Skillful facilitation of PSC workshops is akin to disciplined improvisation, in which facilitators must balance structure and flexibility in order to scaffold teachers' learning. Although in many ways facilitation of PD is similar to leading classroom lessons, working with adult learners is considerably different from teaching K–12 students, and as such, it requires new knowledge and skills on the part of teacher leaders. By taking part in a carefully organized and purposeful MLP program, teacher leaders can acquire and hone their facilitation skills and become masterful leaders of PSC workshops. In addition, the MLP serves as an ongoing resource for teacher leaders to connect with one another, share their experiences, collaboratively plan PSC workshops, and devise solutions to any challenging situations that arise.

Summer Leadership Academy

A Summer Leadership Academy is the first component of the MLP model. The academy is typically a multiday affair; we have most commonly run the academies over 3–5 days during the summer when school is not in session. The academies are meant for both new and returning PSC facilitators. They can be held yearly as an opportunity for learning about and/or reflecting on PSC workshops and associated components.

As they plan for a Summer Leadership Academy, MLP leaders either select the PSC problems that they want the teacher leaders to use during the two cycles of the PSC during the upcoming school year or they select a variety of possible problems and have the teacher leaders provide input about which ones they want to use. Additionally, the MLP leaders either create teacher-analysis tasks in advance (as described in Chapter 2) or devote a portion of the Summer Academy to generating the teacher-analysis tasks collaboratively with the teacher leaders.

During the initial portion of the Summer Leadership Academy, teacher leaders become acquainted with these PSC math problems and begin to think about how they will teach the problems to their own students prior to conducting their PSC workshops. For example, they brainstorm about whether and how they might modify each problem, depending on the classes they will be teaching and the students who are likely to be in those classes. Then the teacher leaders consider how they will use the teacher-analysis tasks in their PSC workshops, and whether and how those might be modified. Throughout their participation in the Summer Leadership Academy, teacher leaders need to have a voice when it comes to the nature of the upcoming PSC iterations and they must take ownership of the PD process. These initial activities help ensure that this will happen.

When the teacher leaders think about the PSC problems, they are likely to notice an important distinction between their roles as teachers and as facilitators. We refer to this distinction as "wearing two hats": a teacher hat and a facilitator hat. With their teacher hat on, the teacher leaders can consider how their students would approach the problem and how they, as teachers, would use the problem in their classrooms to promote student learning of the relevant math content and practices. With their facilitator hat on, the teacher leaders can consider how to present the problem to other teachers, how to foster productive conversations among the teachers, and how to promote teacher learning of both content and instructional practices.

In order to help the teacher leaders become adept at switching between their teacher and facilitator hats, we have found it beneficial to orchestrate mini-PSC simulations, using the problems selected for the PSC cycles during the upcoming academic year. During these simulations, the teacher leaders can experience both taking part in and leading the various activities that comprise PSC workshops. After they play the role of teachers participating in the PSC, teacher leaders can reflect on their experience and the impact that particular facilitation moves by the MLP leaders had on their learning. When they play the role of facilitators, teacher leaders gain a sense of the planning that is needed to carry out specific activities, and they get the opportunity to rehearse those activities and reflect on their own facilitation moves. In this way, the complexity of facilitating PSC workshops can be both broken down and systematically examined within a supportive environment.

Initial Summer Leadership Academy. When teacher leaders take part in their first Summer Leadership Academy, they are introduced to the objectives and principles that underlie the PSC model, along with the mechanics of running PSC workshops. An important resource in this respect is the PSC Facilitator's Guide (see cset.stanford.edu/psc). This guide was developed by our research team and provides detailed descriptions and rationales for the different activities that make up each PSC workshop. The PSC Facilitator's Guide also offers information and guidance about the types of decisions that facilitators typically make as they prepare for and conduct each workshop. It includes a variety of vignettes and examples from our own experiences developing the PSC model and conducting workshops.

Another unique component of the initial Summer Leadership Academy involves creating a plan for how to introduce the PSC to the group of teachers with whom the teacher leaders expect to work, assuming that those teachers are unfamiliar with the model. When introducing the PSC to teachers (as well as to other invested players, such as school principals and administrators), it is critical for teacher leaders to be able to clearly articulate the core features of the model and what teachers can expect to do and learn in PSC workshops, and for the leaders to have strategies for garnering support.

Typically, teacher leaders begin to familiarize the teachers at their school with the PSC by holding what we call a "PSC Workshop 0." This workshop serves as a preparatory meeting to help ensure that the teachers are on board, that they understand what the PSC entails, and that they see the potential for the PSC workshops to provide a constructive and enjoyable learning experience. In general, Workshop 0 focuses on building a professional community in which teachers become comfortable working on mathematical problems together, examining video from one another's mathematics lessons, and collaboratively analyzing student thinking and mathematics instruction. A more extensive description of this workshop and suggestions for facilitating it can be found in the PSC Facilitator's Guide.

Subsequent Summer Leadership Academies. In our experience, it is extremely fruitful for MLP leaders to hold an annual Summer Leadership Academy, even after teacher leaders have gained familiarity with and experience facilitating the PSC. As noted above, one set of activities each summer includes selecting and/or modifying the PSC problems and teacher-analysis tasks for the upcoming year, and beginning to plan the lessons that the teacher leaders will teach to their own students using the PSC problems. In addition, in some cases, there may be new teacher leaders joining the group, and the Summer Leadership Academy provides these novices with the opportunity to learn from their more experienced colleagues. For returning teacher leaders, the Summer Leadership Academy is an opportunity to revisit and refine their facilitation skills. Just as learning about and improving teaching is a career-long endeavor, the development of effective facilitation skills benefits from dedicated, ongoing collaborative learning and support. During annual Summer Leadership Academies, experienced teacher leaders can share and reflect upon their facilitation the previous year as they begin to plan for their upcoming PSC workshops. When they take part in activities such as role-playing and simulations, with the guidance of the MLP leader and feedback from their colleagues, teacher leaders can actively deconstruct and seek to improve designated aspects of their leadership practice.

Leader Support Meetings

As part of the MLP model, prior to each PSC workshop that a teacher leader will facilitate, he or she attends a Leader Support Meeting, along with other PSC teacher leaders in the district. There, participants receive structured guidance as they plan for their upcoming workshops. Thus, in a given PSC iteration, there are three Leader Support Meetings, as shown in Figure 6.1. The meetings include time for the teacher leaders to work collaboratively, to share ideas and concerns, to rehearse the PSC activities they are planning, and to receive feedback from one another and the MLP leaders. During the academic year's Leader Support Meetings, the teacher leaders most often don their facilitator hats and zero in on preparing to engage other teachers in the focal activities of the various PSC workshops—including working through the mathematical content, analyzing student thinking, and examining instructional practices.

In addition to addressing the specific components of each PSC workshop, the Leader Support Meetings offer opportunities for the teacher leaders to continually reflect upon whether the focus of their PD is consonant with the interests and goals of the teachers with whom they are working. As a group, the teacher leaders can share ideas for tailoring their workshops to meet specific needs and brainstorm solutions to concerns that range from pragmatic (e.g., logistical and organizational constraints) to ideological (e.g., integrating other school or district foci into the PSC). Mirroring the development of community among the teachers in a PSC group, ideally the teacher leaders who take part in the MLP will form a productive learning community, serving as resources and sounding boards for one another.

Leader Support Meeting 1. In the same way that teachers must be able to support their students as they work through and learn from a mathematical problem, teacher leaders must be able to support teachers' work on the selected PSC problem in Workshop 1. Therefore, during the first Leader Support Meeting, the teacher leaders spend the majority of their time thinking about how to help their group of teachers deeply understand the problem in order to use it effectively with their students. For example, the teacher leaders might break into small groups and take turns facilitating selected portions of the workshop, such as introducing the teacher-analysis task or leading a discussion based on the task. Through this type of activity, teacher leaders gain experience engaging in topics such as the following:

- Prompting teachers to think deeply about the relevant mathematics in the problem
- Guiding teachers to generate multiple representations and multiple solution strategies that are likely to be useful in their instruction on the problem
- Encouraging teachers to analyze the pros and cons of the various representations and strategies, along with their mathematical relationships and connections

The teacher leaders typically teach a lesson with the selected PSC problem in at least one of their own classes and videotape that lesson prior to the first Leader Support Meeting. Then, during the meeting, the teacher leaders share their experiences implementing the problem, including aspects of their lesson that went well, unexpected challenges they encountered, student solution strategies that were both anticipated and unanticipated, and ways they would modify either their lesson or the problem. Reflecting on their own classroom experiences and hearing about their colleagues' experiences using the same problem builds a knowledge base from which the facilitators can draw during their upcoming workshops with teachers, enabling them to pinpoint potentially troublesome aspects of the problem for both teachers and students that might not have been addressed in the Summer Leadership Academy.

Another important component of the first Leader Support Meeting is exploring ways to assist teachers in adapting the PSC problem for the particular students in their classes, in order to meet the diverse needs of all learners. Similarly, teacher leaders consider how they can help teachers fit the problem into their specific curricular and learning goals, and how they might highlight connections to the CCSSM or other relevant standards. Activities that we have found to be particularly useful in this regard include working with the teacher leaders to identify the math content standards at each grade level aligned with the problem, discussing the various representations and solution strategies that are both atypical and typical, and predicting the math practices that the problem is likely to elicit.

Additionally, as part of the first Leader Support Meeting, teacher leaders contemplate how to create a PD environment in which teachers are comfortable exploring the mathematics addressed in the PSC problem. During the meeting, teacher leaders brainstorm and discuss strategies for ensuring that the teachers in their group will be willing to publicly display their mathematical knowledge, including their strengths and limitations related to the content at hand. An important role that teacher leaders prepare for is prompting the teachers in their groups to think carefully about the challenges of using the selected problem in their classrooms. We have also found it valuable to discuss how they will handle the situation when a teacher displays a mathematical error or misconception. As a group, the teacher leaders can learn from and support one another in their efforts to build professional communities in which teachers eagerly share mathematical ideas, acknowledge areas in which they struggle, and jointly build their mathematical knowledge for teaching.

Leader Support Meetings 2 and 3. Teacher leaders attend the second and third Leader Support Meetings prior to facilitating PSC Workshops 2 and 3, respectively. These meetings provide opportunities for the teacher leaders to plan and practice leading discussions about student reasoning and instructional practices based on the teachers' implementation of the PSC problem. Because video clips from the participating teachers' lessons are such an integral part of PSC Workshops 2 and 3, a critical challenge for facilitators lies in the selection of clips. Ideally, teacher leaders will come to Leader Support Meetings 2 and 3 with video and other classroom artifacts they have collected from their group of teachers. Then, together with their colleagues and the MLP leaders, the teacher leaders can review the videos, select short clips to use in their upcoming workshops, and craft discussion questions that match their selections.

A significant portion of time in the second and third Leader Support Meetings is typically devoted to looking through the available video, in small groups and/or as a whole group, in order to choose the best options and to plan discussions around those choices. Going through the process of identifying video clips, and assisting their colleagues in this regard, promotes teacher leaders' knowledge about the features of "rich" video clips, including determining which clips are most likely to lead to productive PD conversations. To assist teacher leaders in selecting clips, we created a "video clip selection matrix," as shown in Figure 6.2. This matrix describes the types of clips that are likely to be effective for PSC Workshops 2 and 3, organized by where the situation depicted in the clip typically would occur in a lesson (i.e., in the introduction, development, or summary components of the lesson).

Toward the end of the iPSC project, our research team encouraged the teacher leaders to give this video clip selection matrix to the teachers in their groups and have them select possible clips from their own videotaped lessons to show during the upcoming PSC workshops. The teacher leaders then came to the Leader Support Meetings with a set of clip possibilities. They still had to spend a considerable amount of time watching the possible clips and determining the best options.

Figure 6.2. PSC Video Clip Selection Matrix

PSC Workshop	Introduction of the Problem	Development of Lesson	Summary of Lesson
Workshop 2: Student Thinking	Clip(s) showing student ideas as the problem is introduced (e.g., variety of initial ideas, prior knowledge, misconceptions)	Clip(s) showing student(s) grappling with the problem (e.g., naïve or atypical solutions, misconceptions, unique representations); clip(s) of students in a small group debating two or more different solutions to the problem	Clip(s) showing students sharing their ideas at the end of the lesson—focusing on a single idea or range of ideas (e.g., strategies used, questions remaining)
Workshop 3: Teacher's Role	Clip(s) showing how the teacher(s) introduced the problem to their students (e.g., modification of the problem, bringing in prior knowledge, guided questioning, very open-ended); clip(s) showing students interpreting and discussing the problem after it is introduced (e.g., variety of initial ideas, prior knowledge misconceptions, language issues)	Clip(s) showing the teacher talking to the whole class (e.g., pulling the class together during a lesson to address a common misconception); clip(s) showing the teacher interacting with a small group or individual students (e.g., asking questions to a group of students during small-group activity, asking an individual student to explain his or her work)	Clip(s) showing the teacher's role in the summary (e.g., providing a summary, interacting with presenting students, facilitating a class discussion about students' solutions)

As they take part in the Leader Support Meetings, PSC facilitators gain important insights about identifying video and artifacts that can anchor their workshops, collaboratively brainstorm and rehearse a variety of facilitation strategies designed to bring out teachers' ideas, and receive feedback about their choices for clips and facilitation strategies. Rehearsals of video-based discussions are a particularly useful activity in preparing for Workshops 2 and 3, as this aspect of PSC facilitation is a new experience for many of the teacher leaders. In some of our Leader Support Meetings, for example, we ask individual teacher leaders or teacher leader pairs to facilitate a discussion with their colleagues based on a video clip they selected, together with the launching and probing questions they prepared. The other teacher leaders then provide written or oral feedback about their clip choice and the discussion, following a Rehearsal Debrief protocol that we developed for this purpose (see Figure 6.3). Armed with targeted, constructive feedback, the teacher leaders then determine whether and how to modify their workshop plans.

Through these experiences, teacher leaders gain the opportunity to learn about the types of reactions teachers might have to the selected video clips and the accompanying prompts—including what teachers are likely to notice in the video, what they are likely to miss, and the range of comments they might offer. This type of feedback enables teacher leaders to generate realistic expectations and learning goals, fine-tune their launching questions and follow-up probes, and ensure that the conversations in their PSC workshops will go down an intentional path and remain productive.

Additionally, as part of the Leader Support Meetings, teacher leaders gain proficiency in building professional learning communities that will be successful using the PSC model, increase the likelihood of teachers' sustained participation, and foster their commitment to growth and change.

Figure 6.3. Rehearsal Debrief

Feedback for Each Teacher Leader	Teacher Leader: (name)_____	Teacher Leader: (name)_____	Teacher Leader: (name)_____
What goals did the teacher leader appear to have? • What specifically in the discussion makes you think so?			
What clip(s) did the teacher leader show? • How did the clip impact the discussion?			
What facilitation moves did the teacher leader use? • How did these moves impact the discussion?			
What questions did the teacher leader ask? • How did the teacher leader impact the discussion? • What else could have been asked?			

The development of community is a continual process that requires a great deal of thought and planning on the part of facilitators, especially when the PD involves video from the participating teachers' classrooms. During Leader Support Meetings, teacher leaders discuss strategies for establishing and maintaining group norms that will help teachers feel comfortable analyzing video from their peers and having their own videos analyzed.

LEADING THE MLP PROGRAM

Like the PSC, the MLP program should be organized and led by one or more knowledgeable individuals who are invested in the success of the program. In other words, generating a cohort of PSC facilitators and running an MLP program naturally requires a "facilitator educator." The MLP leader should be fluent enough with the design and processes of the PSC to effectively convey the model to teacher leaders and experienced enough as a PD leader to guide novices through the terrain of PD facilitation. Furthermore, the MLP leader must understand the constraints and interests of the local community and envision ways of adapting both the MLP and PSC models to best meet these needs.

In our description of the MLP above, we discussed several facilitation practices that our research team used when we led MLP programs with teacher leaders. In this section, we review these practices and describe some of the ways in which we incorporated them into the MLP meetings, as guidance for other MLP leaders. (The next chapter illustrates many of the practices in action through a series of vignettes drawn from one of our MLP programs.) The MLP leaders from our research team intentionally used the following practices when they facilitated the Summer Leadership Academy and Leader Support Meetings:

- Fostering in-depth discussions
- Modeling followed by reflection
- Rehearsals or simulations
- Metacognition and self-reflection
- Individualized coaching

It is important to facilitate discussions that are meaningful to the teacher leaders based on their current—and often changing—needs and circumstances. For example, when the teacher leaders encountered specific challenges in their PSC workshops, such as teachers who are reluctant to implement a PSC problem, we addressed these obstacles by drawing on the combined knowledge of the teacher leaders as a group. Through these discussions, teacher leaders had the opportunity to gain an understanding of how to facilitate similar conversations in their PSC workshops.

   MLP leaders can model the types of activities and facilitation practices that teacher leaders would be likely to use in their own PSC workshops. For example, when we conducted Summer Leadership Academies, we modeled how to plan and conduct video-based discussions. In addition, we modeled specific strategies for promoting community, responding to teachers' mathematical errors, and adapting the PD to meet the goals and perceived needs of the participating teachers. Perhaps more important, we asked the teacher leaders to reflect on those activities and facilitation practices, in order to highlight them and make explicit our intentions.

   We also included opportunities for rehearsals and simulations throughout the MLP, so that teacher leaders could gain experience and confidence leading the various types of PSC activities. During these rehearsals, teacher leaders had the opportunity to practice specific components of their upcoming PSC workshops, such as leading discussions about the teacher-analysis tasks or selected video clips, and they had the opportunity to consider other teacher leaders' facilitation of the same components. The teacher leaders we worked with found the rehearsals of video-based discussions to be especially valuable, because most of them had not experienced such discussions as either participants in or leaders of previous PD workshops.

   Additionally, we encouraged the teacher leaders to engage in metacognitive strategies, such as reflecting on their own thought processes as they participated in the MLP meetings. As MLP leaders, we modeled this process of metacognition by talking with the teacher leaders about our own goals, why we designed the MLP activities in a particular manner, and how we thought the activities were working out so far. Because teacher leaders play dual roles, as both leaders and learners, we asked them to "wear one hat at a time," and we frequently prompted them to attend carefully to their thinking about the PSC and the facilitation of PD workshops, both when they were participating in the activities we led and when they were planning their upcoming workshops.

   Finally, the MLP model also includes coaching for individual teacher leaders as needed. Similar in many respects to coaching classroom teachers, coaching teacher leaders can be a means of providing personalized support in areas where there are notable concerns or struggles, or where an advocate is needed. The teacher leaders with whom we worked often turned to the MLP leaders to seek advice on difficult or unexpected situations, or to address areas in their facilitation that they wanted to improve. On some occasions, the MLP leaders attended the teacher leaders' PSC workshops, in order to gain insights into a unique group of teachers and local circumstances and to offer specific guidance to help ensure that the teacher leaders found success with the PSC model. For instance, if a teacher leader noted that his or her group of teachers was struggling with the problem or that the workshop was getting derailed because of other issues within the school, an MLP leader would come by to help facilitate, to address the teachers' concerns, and to debrief with the teacher leader at the conclusion of the workshop.

THE DEGREE OF FLEXIBILITY BUILT INTO THE MLP

As we noted at the beginning of the chapter, the MLP, like the PSC, is designed to be a flexible model, easily adapted to the unique circumstances and constraints of the context in which it is being implemented. MLP leaders can decide, for example, the number of days to include in the Summer Leadership Academy and whether to preselect the PSC problems or have the PSC facilitators collaboratively decide from among a set of possible problems the MLP leaders provide. The MLP leaders decide which activities and facilitation practices to model in the Leader Support Meetings and which activities the facilitators should rehearse. As designers of this model, we did not attempt to identify all of the possible variations or all the ways in which the Summer Leadership Academy and Leader Support Meetings might evolve over the duration of a PD program. We look forward to hearing from other MLP leaders about their own experiences in implementing the MLP model and adapting it to the goals and needs of the PSC facilitators with whom they work.

CHAPTER 7

The MLP Model in Action

We use vignettes in this chapter to illustrate what the Math Leadership Preparation model looks like in practice. The vignettes are drawn from the Summer Leadership Academy and a set of Leader Support Meetings that took place during Year 3 of the iPSC project. Karen, a coauthor of this book and a member of our research team, led the Summer Leadership Academy and Leader Support Meetings in collaboration with Joanie, the secondary mathematics coordinator of our partner school district. Other members of the research team participated in the meetings and assisted with small-group activities. Eight mathematics teacher leaders from six middle schools attended the meetings, including three returning teacher leaders and five new teacher leaders.

THE SUMMER LEADERSHIP ACADEMY: CREATING A BROAD PLAN USING THE FUEL GAUGE PROBLEM

We begin by presenting a series of vignettes that depict selected components of the Summer Leadership Academy. This particular Summer Leadership Academy was conducted over a 5-day period and was the longest summer academy that our research team conducted. As described in Chapter 6, the MLP model is adaptable to the local context. As an example, Summer Leadership Academies can be held for shorter periods of time; we have conducted them for as short a period as 2½ days. The vignettes highlight two foci that are typical of PSC summer leadership academies—doing mathematics with teachers and facilitating video-based discussions.

Preparing Teacher Leaders to Do Math with Teachers

As noted in Chapter 6, during the Summer Leadership Academy teacher leaders begin to think carefully about the PSC problems and teacher-analysis tasks they will use with their teachers during the upcoming academic year. PSC problems may be preselected by the MLP leaders (as was most often the case in the iPSC project), or teachers might be given several problems from which to choose. In this chapter, we highlight portions of the academy in which the teacher leaders were preparing to conduct PSC workshops using the Fuel Gauge Problem. The Fuel Gauge Problem is a rate-and-ratio problem adapted from Jacob and Fosnot (2008). It requires solvers to determine how many miles Frank can drive given how much gas he has left in his truck (see Figure 7.1).

   Doing the math wearing their teacher hats. In the Summer Leadership Academy, the teacher leaders first become acquainted with this problem while wearing their "teacher hats." Because the teacher leaders will use this problem in their own classrooms during the upcoming school year, thinking it through initially as teachers (rather than as PSC facilitators) seems to be a natural starting point. To accompany the Fuel Gauge Problem, the MLP leaders created a teacher-analysis task (shown in Figure 7.2), which lists four potential student solution strategies. To begin the activity, they distribute the Fuel Gauge Problem and the teacher-analysis task to the group.

The teacher leaders move into small groups that have at least one novice and one returning facilitator and begin working on the Fuel Gauge Problem and accompanying teacher-analysis task. One group—consisting of Sarah (a PhD student on the iPSC project), Kaitlyn (a novice teacher leader), and Mandy (a returning teacher leader)—decides to work individually to solve the problem using any method each wants, and then to talk through the strategies listed

Figure 7.1. Fuel Gauge Problem

Frank runs a business called Frank's Fresh Farm Produce. Once a week, he drives north of the city to farms where he buys the best possible fresh produce for his customers. Frank can travel 600 miles on a full tank of gas. His truck has a fancy, accurate fuel gauge.

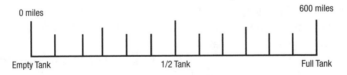

Usually, Frank has time to visit only one farm on each trip, but one week he decides to visit both Stan's and Louisa's farms. When Frank drives from his store to Stan's farm and back, he knows he will use 5/12 of a tank of gas. When he drives to Louisa's farm and back, he uses 1/3 of a tank. From a map of the area, he learns that there is a road from Stan's farm to Louisa's farm that is 120 miles long. He realizes that he can drive from his store to Stan's farm, then to Louisa's farm, and then back to his store in one loop.

   Frank can tell by looking at his fuel gauge that he has 5/8 of a tank of gas. Can he drive this loop without having to stop for fuel? Or should he buy gas before he starts his trip?

Figure 7.2. Fuel Gauge Problem Teacher-Analysis Task

Below are some strategies for solving this problem. For each strategy, explain a student solution method or methods, and the possible student interpretation of that method. Describe potential challenges with each method.

1. Using the representation (gas gauge) and marking distances
2. Working with everything in miles
3. Working with fractions of a gas tank
4. Blending approaches such as combining 5/24 + 1/6 with a common whole of 24 to get 9/24

in the teacher-analysis task. Once everyone has finished working the problem on her own, the group comes together to share their thinking.

Sarah comments, "If the analysis task hadn't given us the different strategies, I might not have seen them as different ways to solve the problem. I used kind of a blended approach where I focused on what each individual fraction represented."

Kaitlyn shares her strategy, explaining, "I was trying to mark the numbers on the gauge, but I had to remember to cut the round-trips in half. 5/12 became 2.5/12. So I marked that on the gauge. Then 1/3 is 4/12, and half of that is 2/12. I marked that, so now I'm at 4.5/12. But then you have to add in the 120 miles."

Mandy offers, "It's 225 miles, not including the 120 miles from Stan to Louisa."

Kaitlyn laughingly agrees. "Right. But it's weird you looked at it that way."

Mandy explains further: "Well, when I tried to find the number of miles, I marked on the gauge how much gas it would take to do half of the round-trips, to Stan and to Louisa, and it totaled 225 miles. Then I had to add in 120 miles. I decided just to round that to 125, so the total comes to 350. And I can see on the gauge that's 7/12 of a tank. So I knew he had enough gas."

The group considers whether it is easier to solve the problem by thinking about the trip in terms of the number of miles that must be driven or as fractions of the fuel that will be expended.

Kaitlyn reflects, "When I was looking at the fuel tank, it seemed easier to first use the gauge as fractions and then think in miles."

Sarah points out that there are many possible common denominators one could choose when solving the problem based on fractions. She proposes, "You could use 24ths. Or 120ths. Or even 600ths." The teachers try solving the problem again using these denominators.

As a side note, Sarah suggests, "I am thinking the kids will need a visualization of what they are doing. They need to see the whole loop Frank will travel to understand what calculations to do."

Kaitlyn nods and says, "Yes, I would have the kids draw the route." Then she returns to the strategy that was most comfortable to her and notes, "I liked doing the problem in miles rather than fractions. Since the whole tank was 600 miles, I knew that half a tank was 300 and a fourth of a tank was 150. That means each tick mark on the fuel gauge was 50 miles. So going from Stan's farm and back is 5/12, which is 250 miles, and half of that is 125. The trip to Louisa's is 1/3, which is 100 miles, and I had to cut that in half. So I added 125, 100, and 120 and got 345. And I knew 5/8 of a tank is between the seven and eight twelfths marks on the fuel gauge. So he has enough gas for 375 miles, which is more than enough."

As they review and share their approaches to the Fuel Gauge Problem, Sarah, Kaitlyn, and Mandy acknowledge the complexity of the mathematics content, discuss the different strategies they came up with, and make sure they are comfortable with each possible strategy. They then turn their attention to thinking about some of the challenges their students might face when given the problem. This initial experience with the problem prompts enthusiastic conversations among all of the small groups of teacher leaders, and sets a foundation to consider how they might engage in the math with their teachers.

Doing the math wearing their facilitator hats. Now that the group has become acquainted with the Fuel Gauge Problem and teacher-analysis task, the MLP leaders shift gears and ask the teacher leaders put on their "facilitator hats" in order to prepare for their upcoming PSC workshops. Based on their experience working through the teacher-analysis task, the teacher leaders talk with one another and begin brainstorming how they might introduce the problem to their teachers.

Karen begins, "Now we are going to reflect on your experience with the teacher-analysis task. How did that help you think about the mathematics of the problem? How will you use this task with the teachers? How will you launch it?"

Kaitlyn starts, "I like the teacher-analysis task, and I think my teachers will, too. It really makes you think in different ways."

Sarah agrees, "Yeah. It's an easy way to get teachers to focus on students' thinking by analyzing the different strategies."

"Could we give the teachers one solution at a time to analyze and discuss as a whole group?" wonders Mandy.

"I think that would be a nice way to start. That way, we would have more control over the discussion maybe," adds Kaitlyn.

"But do you want to control the discussion? Why not let them explore the different solutions any way they want to? What do you guys think?" asks Sarah.

Mandy chimes in, "I think we could do it either way. Letting teachers explore, some will just go down the page randomly, and others might do the strategies that resonate with them the most. But, since we are just starting out, I think it makes sense to go in an order that is planned by us. We might be more prepared to anticipate questions and issues working problem by problem."

Karen, one of the academy leaders, reframes the conversation and asks the groups to come together to debrief and consider the affordances of the teacher-analysis task. Mandy says, "The analysis task is great because it helps us show our teachers all the ways that kids think about the problem. And it asks them to do the analysis."

Robert adds, "I agree. Also, the analysis itself makes them have a deeper understanding of the mathematics. It also brings out the gaps and holes that our students might have."

With their facilitator hats on, the teacher leaders carefully consider how to use the teacher-analysis task and why it will be a helpful exercise for their teachers. They acknowledge that there are different ways to engage their groups in working on the Fuel Gauge Problem and recognize the importance of anticipating how conversations about the problem might unfold. This process of working on the problem through both a teacher and a facilitator lens supports the teacher leaders' mathematical knowledge for teaching as well as their mathematical knowledge for facilitating professional development.

Preparing Teacher Leaders to Facilitate Video-Based Discussions

Another salient component of the Summer Leadership Academy is to prepare the teacher leaders to facilitate conversations based on video clips of the selected PSC problem. In the Year 3 Summer Leadership Academy, the MLP leaders elected to show video of the Fuel Gauge Problem from a lesson taught by a member of the research team, Rachael. In this case, Rachael had taught the problem to a class of 6th-graders, most of whom were English language learners (ELLs). Watching the video clip enables the teacher leaders to see how the Fuel Gauge Problem was used in an actual classroom and allows them to think about the problem from both a teacher and a facilitator perspective.

Analyzing video wearing their teacher hats. First, the teacher leaders analyze the clip wearing their teacher hats, carefully considering Rachael's introduction.

Before playing the video, Karen frames the teacher leaders' viewing by explaining, "Rachael has just introduced the problem to her students at this point. They have gone through the vocabulary, and she has decided that they have a good grasp of the problem. The guiding question for this viewing is: How is Rachael scaffolding the mathematics and using representations from the problem as a resource for the students?"

The clip shows Rachael sitting in a chair at the front of the room with her students seated on the floor around her. Next to Rachael is a large sheet of chart paper with the fuel gauge drawn at the top and three circles arranged in a triangle, as shown in Figure 7.3. The circles are labeled "Frank," "Stan," and "Louisa."

> Rachael begins by pointing to the fuel gauge and asking, "So, here is Frank's gas gauge. How many miles can he drive when his tank is full? There is something on the diagram that tells you."
> Student A answers, "600 miles?"
> Rachael replies, "Good. So how far could he drive on half a tank?"
> Student B responds, "300 miles."
> Rachael continues, "How far on a quarter of a tank? Talk to your partner for a second."
> After the students chat with a partner, Student C responds, "150 miles."
> Rachael asks, "How did you get that?" to which Student C replies, "Because 150 and 150 equals 300."
> Rachael again points to the fuel gauge and asks, "So you are thinking this is 150 and another 150 here is 300. So how far could he get on three-fourths of a tank?"
> Student D states, "450, because 300 plus 150 equals 450."

As is common in PSC workshops, the teacher leaders watch the clip twice. Prior to the second viewing, Karen reminds them to consider how Rachael scaffolded the mathematics for her English language learners.

Carla remarks, "She started with the obvious and went to the next obvious, and moved the kids along."

Kaitlyn adds, "She also asked for an explanation of how they got to 150, and I think that building on that explanation helped them get to ¾ of a tank."

Figure 7.3. Rachael's Drawing

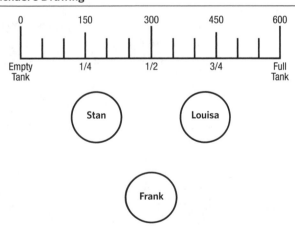

Mandy points out, "I noticed the way she used different types of responses. She started with the whole class, and then as the questions got harder, she had them discuss with a partner. I think that allowed access for other students."

Many others contribute to the conversation before Karen concludes, "We wanted to show you Rachael's approach to resizing this problem for 6th-grade ELLs. Although she gave a lot of scaffolding, when she finishes her launch these students still have a lot of questions to resolve. This is an important point to consider: How do you provide scaffolding and other tools for diverse groups of students, but still leave the problem open for inquiry and open for multiple solution strategies? This is something we'll keep talking about and it is a good segue into the next part of our academy."

By watching and discussing Rachael's video clip, the teacher leaders have the opportunity to engage in the PSC in the same manner as the teachers in their own workshops. Because they are also teachers, it is natural for them to attend to the pertinent instructional issues that come up in the video. Opportunities to wear their teacher hats, especially around classroom video, are likely to be highly engaging and at the same time serve as a model for when they need to shift into the facilitator role.

Analyzing video wearing their facilitator hats. After they have engaged with Rachael's video clip from their perspective as teachers, the group shifts to thinking about how they might use the same clip if they were facilitating their own PSC workshops. In particular, they consider how they might guide teachers' conversations about the clip in a particular direction, toward an identified instructional or mathematical goal.

Joanie [the co-MLP facilitator] tells the group, "Let's consider how we might use this clip from Rachael's classroom with your teachers. What might your instructional or mathematical goal be?"

Carla jumps in: "I think I would want to discuss ways to scaffold the problem. I think it's an important idea to reach more kids. Rachael did a great job scaffolding for her ELLs, so there are a lot of opportunities for teachers to notice the different scaffolds."

"I completely agree," adds Kaitlyn.

Jordan presses, "I think I would want them to talk about the different ways that representations can support student learning. Rachael does a nice job using the fuel gauge and I do not think the teachers at my school use double number lines. (A double number line represents two different quantities by using one scale on the top number line and a different scale on the bottom number line. In this case, one scale represents miles and the other scale represents the amount of gas in the gas tank.) I think my teachers would really benefit from discussing all the representations that Rachael used. They really help the kids 'see' the problem."

Robert adds, "I can see using this clip to have a conversation about the different ways we might launch this problem depending on the grade level. That is the beauty of video. We can analyze Rachael's approach and other approaches. As Karen and Joanie would say, 'We can analyze the "affordances and constraints" of each approach.'"

Joanie asks the teacher leaders to talk with the person sitting next to them about the way that they would use the clip, to make sure that everyone has a chance to share their thoughts.

Next, Karen encourages the teacher leaders to think about what their group of teachers might say about the clip, given the way its viewing is framed. She explains, "So now, everyone has thought about a goal for your conversation based on this video. I've heard people name several, such as thinking about scaffolding or the representations that Rachael used. Now I want you to work with a partner to anticipate the conversation that might unfold with your teachers. There will probably be multiple paths. See if you can anticipate those paths and jot down ways you can push the conversation deeper so it moves beyond a superficial level. For example, if you want to focus on the representations, how can you help the teachers explore them and talk about the pros and cons of using each one?"

In this exchange, the teacher leaders don their facilitator hats and think carefully about how to foster productive conversations with teachers based on a given video clip. The MLP leaders walk them through the process of identifying a goal or purpose for watching the clip, which helps the teacher leaders see that a particular clip can be viewed through a variety of lenses. In addition, the MLP leaders encourage the teacher leaders to anticipate what teachers might say about a given clip, given the lens they have chosen, so that they can be better prepared to facilitate and ask probing questions. As noted in Chapter 2, teacher leaders might identify their goals for a workshop first and then select video that has the potential to foster discussions focused on that goal. Or they might first select a video clip and then decide on a goal. In the example above, we used the latter approach so that the teacher leaders could grapple with a common video clip but generate individual goals.

Selecting video clips and planning video-based discussions. Next, with their facilitator hats still on, the teacher leaders begin thinking about the process of *selecting* video clips and planning video-based discussions. To do this, they look through the chapter on Workshop 2 in the PSC Facilitator's Guide (available from cset.stanford.edu/psc), jot down some initial ideas about conducting their own Workshop 2 using the Fuel Gauge

Problem, and engage in a conversation about choosing and using video in PSC workshops.

Karen asks, "What makes a good video clip, based on your reading and also watching some clips?"

Carla begins, "A good clip lends itself to discussion. For example, we see something that teachers or students do that could go in several directions from that point. That's a good place in a lesson for pausing the video, predicting what might happen, and then seeing what the teacher actually did and reflecting on that."

Robert expands on Carla's comment, saying, "I like that idea. Then the discussion goes from being what the teacher did to being about what else you could do. When would you do that? Why would you do it? And that tends to help with objectivity, not making it personal."

Candace offers, "Another good clip would be where kids are heading in the wrong direction. And looking at how the teacher handled that."

Jordan follows up on Candace's idea: "Actually, for a clip like that, it would be great to stop the video before the teacher intervenes, to think about different strategies. You know, think about what you would do if you were presented with this situation. Don't put the teacher on the spot by showing what they did, especially in your first few workshops."

After this conversation, the teacher leaders split into small groups, watch a 20-minute section of video from Rachael's Fuel Gauge Problem lesson, pick at least one clip, and craft guiding questions that could be used in a hypothetical PSC Workshop 2. They then meet back together as a whole group and share their selections. The idea here is for the teacher leaders to get practice selecting and framing clips and to receive feedback from the larger group regarding their selections.

Kaitlyn, Robert, and Hilda volunteer to share their selection with the full group. Kaitlyn describes the clip they chose and relays their guiding questions: "Given the way the teacher launched the problem, does the launch steer the students to solve it using a particular strategy? What strategy was it? Was it intentional on the teacher's part?"

Karen plays the clip, which shows Rachael launching the problem and asking her students what half of a round-trip means. She prompts the group, "Think about using this clip in your workshop, as well as the guiding question."

After viewing the clip, Mandy brings up some concerns: "I personally think it's too long. I think it could be scaled down and have a more focused question. I'm also not sure about the last question about intentionality. The teacher did so many different things in this 5-minute clip. I think that's a hard question to answer. I would ask something more specific like, 'This teacher introduced the idea of a "round-trip." How does that affect the students' thinking?'"

Others agree that asking about the videotaped teacher's intentions is problematic.

Kaitlyn notes, "I'm not sure you can tell whether it's intentional. And why does that even matter?"

Jordan cautions, "If I were the teacher, I would get defensive. The question has to be very carefully worded."

After a few more minutes of discussion, the group comes up with the following revised guiding question: What mathematical pathways might this launch set the students on? The teacher leaders agree that this question focuses viewers on the same issues as the original question, but is shorter and potentially less judgmental.

Watching a relatively long, 20-minute segment of video in order to select a relatively short clip and then generating ideas about how to frame a discussion about the clip mimics the process that teacher leaders will go through when they are preparing for their own PSC Workshops 2 and 3. Similar to the development of community within PSC workshops, we found the process of providing each group with specific feedback and carefully worded constructive criticism about their clips and questions to be beneficial not only in developing the teacher leaders' facilitation skills, but also in establishing their cohesion as a group of leaders working toward a common goal.

LEADER SUPPORT MEETING 1:
PLANNING FOR PSC WORKSHOP 1 USING THE FUEL GAUGE PROBLEM

After the Summer Leadership Academy, the teacher leaders attend a series of Leader Support Meetings during the fall semester and lead one full iteration of PSC workshops (see Chapter 6). Then, at the start of the spring semester, they meet again in preparation for their second full iteration of PSC workshops using the Fuel Gauge Problem. All of the teacher leaders have taught the Fuel Gauge Problem to their own students. They come to the first Leader Support Meeting fresh from those experiences and with their notes from the Summer Leadership Academy. The purpose of this initial Leader Support Meeting is to ensure that the teacher leaders are well prepared to lead a PSC workshop focused on the mathematics of the Fuel Gauge Problem and are ready to support the teachers at their schools in using the problem with their own students. The MLP leaders have planned the meeting with an eye toward helping the teacher leaders effectively guide their groups to address the mathematical challenges or roadblocks that students are likely to encounter.

Identifying Student Roadblocks Wearing Their Teacher Hats

For the initial activity, the MLP leaders once again encourage the teacher leaders to wear their teacher hats and identify any aspects of the Fuel Gauge Problem that were difficult for their own students. They ask the teacher leaders to rework the problem using the two main solution strategies (miles and fractions) and to pinpoint specific mathematical challenges within each strategy.

Karen tells the teacher leaders that they will spend much of their meeting time brainstorming student difficulties with the Fuel Gauge Problem. She explains, "We want you to be really detailed in your planning for Workshop 1 and in working through the math with your teachers. We want you to solve the problem again, but first solve it using only miles. So, with a partner, work out everything in miles and keep a running list of potential roadblocks that students might run into if they do the problem using miles. What are all of the struggles, challenges, misconceptions, or mistakes they might make?"

After about 30 minutes, the group comes back together to share their ideas. Carla goes to the whiteboard and draws a fuel gauge, divided into 24ths, as shown in Figure 7.4. She notes that each 24th represents 25 miles and explains how she and her partner used this information to work out everything in miles. In the problem, Frank has 5/8 of a tank of gas, which is equal to "15 sets of 25 miles," or 375 miles. To go to Louisa's farm and back is 1/3 of a tank, which equals "8 sets of 25 miles," but because Frank only needs to drive half that distance, it's "4 sets of 25 miles," or 100 miles. To go to Stan's farm and back is 5/12 of a tank, which is "10 sets of 25." But again, Frank only needs to go half that distance, which is "5 sets of 25," or 125 miles. Adding the three distances Frank must travel—100+125+120—we get 345 miles. That amount is less than 375 miles, so Frank does have enough gas to make the trip.

Kaitlyn comments, "I am so glad that Carla did the problem this way! When I did it with my kids, we totally ignored the gauge. We took the 600 and went with that. But when I think back, there were a couple of kids who were breaking it down like she did, looking at what each measure on the gauge was worth."

Figure 7.4. Carla's Fuel Gauge

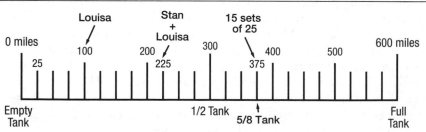

After several other pairs share their strategies, the discussion shifts to a consideration of where students might struggle with the problem if they solve it using miles and how teachers can help them. The MLP leaders create a two-column chart on the whiteboard and act as a scribe for the teacher leaders as they suggest how to fill it in. The first column lists possible roadblocks, and the second column lists ways teachers can address each roadblock. Figure 7.5 displays the completed chart.

Next, the teacher leaders go through a similar process as they rework the problem using fractions. A careful consideration of ways to solve the problem using fractions leads them to include three more potential roadblocks in the chart: adding fractions incorrectly, fraction phobia, and finding a common denominator. For each new roadblock, the group again brainstorms ways to help students. Ideas include using fraction strips, reworking the fuel gauge to be a double number line, and encouraging students to work with only two fractions at a time.

Planning a Discussion of Roadblocks Wearing Their Facilitator Hats

During the next portion of the Leader Support Meeting, the teacher leaders put on their facilitator hats and focus on planning Workshop 1 using the Fuel Gauge Problem. Before the teacher leaders begin to develop

Figure 7.5. Potential Roadblocks When Solving the Fuel Gauge Problem Using Miles

Roadblock	Helping Students Move Past the Roadblock
When working with 12ths for the whole trip, how do we convert the 5/8ths?	• Encourage students to first divide the fuel gauge into fourths, and then into eighths. • Have blank fuel gauges available or a fuel gauge with benchmark fractions marked (i.e., ½, ¼). • Point out that 5/8 is halfway between 4/8 and 6/8.
How do we halve the fractions?	• Encourage students to visually represent the fraction to see what the whole is first, and then divide it in half. • Focus their attention on equivalent fractions. • Go over the meaning of the numerators and denominators. • Refer students back to the fuel gauge and use that as a number line.
What does the 600 miles mean?	• Focus students on the problem context. What do the numbers mean? How do they relate to one another? • Reread the problem. • Connect miles and fractions of a tank.
Should we combine all the distances and then divide them in half?	• Draw a picture of the trip. • Reread the problem, thinking about what "round-trip" means.

concrete written plans, the MLP leaders review the process they just went through together: solving the problem using different strategies, anticipating possible student roadblocks associated with each strategy, and brainstorming ways to support students through those roadblocks. The MLP leaders encourage the teacher leaders to consider planning their workshops using these same basic activities, while also taking into account the teacher leaders' unique school and classroom contexts. After talking and planning in small groups, the teacher leaders come back together and share their ideas.

Kaitlyn and Mandy show the rest of the group a revised Potential Roadblocks chart, to which they have added a third column labeled "Questions to Probe and Move Forward." Kaitlyn explains, "We are thinking we will print out copies of the chart and pass them out to our teachers as we discuss the problem. That way, if we don't have time to discuss each roadblock, the teachers will still have this to refer to. The last column provides teachers with questions they might ask to probe their students."

Mandy continues, "We only have an hour for our Workshop 1. A lot of that time is probably going to get taken up with the math, which is critically important, but there just never seems to be enough time to help the teachers plan. My teachers are really concentrating on the types of questions they want to ask their students. So if we give them something like this chart, it might help them with their lesson planning and to be more successful in teaching the problem."

The other teacher leaders agree that distributing printed copies of this revised chart will be helpful for their teachers as well. Having a written document that lists students' potential struggles along with ways to help them is likely to benefit the teachers not only when they are planning their lessons but also when they are carrying them out, because they can refer to the document as the lesson unfolds. One teacher leader notes that taking the time to prepare various resources for her workshops—such as slides that she shows during the workshop and also sends electronically to her teachers—has always proven to be worthwhile. She explains that the teachers are generally very grateful for her efforts and recognize the commitment she has made to the PSC, which helps reinforce their commitment to the process.

LEADER SUPPORT MEETING 2:
PLANNING FOR PSC WORKSHOP 2 USING THE FUEL GAUGE PROBLEM

Once all of the teacher leaders have conducted Workshop 1 using the Fuel Gauge Problem and several of the teachers in their groups have taught the problem, they attend the second Leader Support Meeting to reflect on their facilitation and plan for their second workshop in the PSC cycle. The teacher leaders all bring video from at least some of their teachers. A central focus of this meeting is the process of selecting clips and preparing guiding questions. Throughout the meeting, the teacher leaders wear their facilitator hats and focus on ensuring that their upcoming workshops will promote meaningful and engaging discussions around video.

Selecting Video Clips and Planning Video-Based Discussions

The MLP leaders begin the meeting by giving the teacher leaders some time to share their experiences conducting Workshop 1 using the Fuel Gauge Problem. They then ask them to think back on their prior experiences leading Workshop 2, especially in terms of choosing video clips that worked well with their groups. This type of reflection activity serves to activate the teacher leaders' memories and primes them to begin picking clips from the Fuel Gauge lessons.

Karen poses the question, "Based on your experiences picking clips so far, what makes a good clip for having productive conversations with your teachers?"

Carla responds, "For me, it was clips that showed student misconceptions. You can really talk about what the students are not understanding and how you as a teacher can address that."

Mandy adds, "I think it needs to be an issue that's not just specific to that problem, but a common math issue that teachers and students will come across again. Not just something like 'round-trip' that is so specific to the Fuel Gauge Problem, but something like a fraction issue that kids always struggle with."

Kaitlyn reacts to Mandy's statement that focusing on the round-trip aspect of the problem is too specific, arguing, "But you could take something like round-trip and generalize it to reading the problem carefully."

Mandy disagrees, saying, "But we want to stay focused on the math!"

Jason defends Kaitlyn's position, using humor to lighten the mood: "Well, I noticed with our kids, their reading sucked! (The group laughs.) If our reading teachers were in that class, they would have had coronaries! They just left everything they were taught in their reading classes. They seemed to think that because they were in a math class, they didn't have to do that."

Karen encourages the group to look at Mandy's and Kaitlyn's ideas as different, but equally valid. She reminds them that they will have the opportunity to use more than one clip and to explore several different issues during their Fuel Gauge Workshops 2 and 3. She proposes, "Mandy's point is that clips that involve student misconceptions should be about important math ideas. Kaitlyn and Jason are raising another important point that's different. I hear you saying that the clip could look at the language in the problem. A lot of our problems that we select do have tricky language in them for kids. It's a big issue for English language learners, and that might be a topic that certain schools want to take up in some of their workshops."

Carla agrees, "At our school, it's an important issue because if the kids don't understand the problem, they'll never get to the math. It's about accessing the problem and thinking about literacy strategies that are specific for mathematics."

Karen summarizes, "So you could pick a clip that shows a misconception about the math or a clip where the student is misinterpreting the problem, or potentially both."

The conversation continues, with the MLP leaders keeping track of the teacher leaders' ideas about what makes a good clip on the whiteboard.

Following this discussion about the features of good video clips, the teacher leaders watch the videos of their teachers using the Fuel Gauge Problem that they brought, select possible clips to show in their upcoming workshops, and review their choices with partners or with the workshop leaders and other members of the research team. Next, the teacher leaders turn their attention to how they will frame the discussion of their selected video clips. After they have picked clips and identified possible questions to launch and guide the discussions, each teacher leader shares at least one video clip and some possible framing questions with the full group. Through this exercise, the teacher leaders receive constructive feedback on how to effectively introduce the clip and guide their teachers through an intentional analysis of it.

A Checklist for Planning PSC Workshops 2 and 3

As they were preparing for this second Leader Support Meeting, the MLP leaders agreed that the teacher leaders would benefit from a checklist indicating the critical decision points related to planning their upcoming PSC Workshops. The MLP leaders created a Checklist for Planning PSC Workshops 2 and 3 (see Figure 7.6), which they decided to distribute to the teacher leaders near the end of the meeting. They go over each bulleted item, pointing out relevant connections to the PSC Facilitator's Guide, suggesting activities they have seen work well in previous PSC workshops, and highlighting several ideas that were already shared in that day's meeting. The MLP leaders encourage the teacher leaders to refer to the checklist as they make final adjustments to their Workshop 2 plans and to keep it as a resource for Workshop 3.

Figure 7.6. Checklist for Planning PSC Workshops 2 and 3

❏ What are your goals for the workshop? How will you articulate your goals to your group?

❏ How will you begin the workshop? (e.g., Reengage the teachers in the problem? Debrief everyone's lesson? Give the teachers a prompt to write about their experiences? Have teachers share in small groups/whole group?)

❏ How will you move into showing videos? (e.g., Review norms for viewing video? Make sure teachers are comfortable with the clips you will show—ask them beforehand?)

❏ How will you introduce each clip? Do you want the teachers to set up their own clips?

❏ What clips will you show? What questions will you ask? Will you show the clips more than once? How much time do you anticipate this will take? Do you have some backup clips, just in case there is more time than expected?

❏ How will you end your workshop? (e.g., Give teachers time to reflect? Ask teachers to consider ways to improve their instruction? Have teachers give feedback?)

❏ For Workshop 2: How will you encourage the teachers to watch their own videos? Will you ask teachers to bring student work to the next meeting? Will you try to gather student work from teachers ahead of time, in order to prepare?

❏ For Workshop 3: How will you end this iteration of the PSC? (e.g., Ask teachers to reflect on what they learned? Ask for their feedback and suggestions for next time?)

LEADER SUPPORT MEETING 3:
PLANNING FOR PSC WORKSHOP 3 USING THE FUEL GAUGE PROBLEM

Teacher leaders attend Leader Support Meeting 3 to prepare for their final PSC workshop using the Fuel Gauge Problem. The MLP leaders begin the meeting by giving the participants some time to journal and reflect on their experiences conducting Workshop 2—in particular, their facilitation of video-based discussions and the depth of the conversations they were able to foster. The teacher leaders share their thoughts and brainstorm ways to have deeper conversations in their workshops, focused on either students' mathematical thinking or teachers' instructional practice.

Then the teacher leaders begin to consider which video clips they want to show in their third PSC workshop. In preparation for this decision, they have collected suggestions from the teachers in their groups who were videotaped teaching the Fuel Gauge Problem. The teacher leaders now must review those suggested video clips and determine which clips they want to show and how best to frame them.

Facilitating Video-Based Discussions

Carla shares with the group a 6-minute video clip that one of her teachers selected, seeking advice on whether and how to make the clip shorter and what sort of guiding question(s) she might ask. Carla's colleagues advise her to use only the first minute of the clip, noting that the modified clip can initiate a conversation about either the students' thinking or the teacher's instructional moves (or both). The shorter clip shows a teacher helping a group of four boys after they have spent some time working through the Fuel Gauge Problem. The boys are trying to piece together several components of the problem, including adding fractions of the fuel tank (with different denominators) and miles traveled, two ideas that are conceptually challenging for them. The group watches the 1-minute clip, brainstorming various possibilities for framing it.

Prior to viewing the clip, Karen reminds the group, "In PSC workshops, we typically foreground either student thinking or teacher instruction, while the other is in the background because the two are naturally intertwined. Let's think about foregrounding either student thinking or instruction."

When the clip is done, Karen asks, "Okay, let's talk about this clip. What do you think should be foregrounded and backgrounded?"

Mandy suggests, "Maybe the clip can be chunked [broken up into smaller clips] so that the teachers can really understand the students' thinking. The chunks would be really short but watching the whole thing is hard, and it seems to go really fast."

Carla responds, "I think I would show the video more than once."

Mandy agrees, saying, "That's a good idea because the conversation about the mathematics and 600 as the total unit is great."

Hilda turns to Mandy and says, "So, Mandy, I heard you say on the side that it would be good for the teachers to try to determine what each student in the group is thinking."

Mandy answers, "Yep. I think you have to do that in the beginning because the kids are at different places with different misconceptions. That's a really good part of this video clip for Carla to use in her workshop. And if you have the students' papers, it would be really good for the teachers to look at them, because it seems like there is a lot of good stuff written down."

Karen pushes the group to think about the video using an instructional lens by asking, "So, it sounds like most of you think Carla should have a student-focused frame for this video, particularly in the beginning. But is there the potential to discuss teacher instruction, too?"

Mandy cautions, "I think if you focus on the teacher actions and how the teacher responds to the students, you have to be incredibly careful because you do not want to put the volunteer teacher out there. You need to be thoughtful in how you approach it."

Joanie offers, "Well, if you stop the video before we know what the teacher *actually* did and ask the group what they *might* do if they were in this situation, you can avoid that personal issue."

Robert proposes, "Once you get the student thinking on the table, then the question about what the teacher might do or what options the teacher has is a good next question."

Karen agrees, "I like the word *options* because it allows the teachers to brainstorm different ways to respond to these students."

Joanie continues, "And this is great for the teacher who is sharing the video because she is getting a lot of feedback and she knows what she did. So it's really good for everyone."

This activity not only gives the teacher leaders time to select clips, but also provides a forum for them to share their burgeoning expertise in facilitating PSC workshops with their colleagues. As we see from the exchange above, the teacher leaders are highly attentive to the dynamics within their groups of teachers. They easily make predictions about how teachers might respond to particular clips, and then they use these predictions to consider the effects of different ways to frame the viewing of video and the subsequent discussion.

Rehearsing Video-Based Conversations and Planning for Workshop 3

After all the teacher leaders have selected at least one video clip and thought about possible guiding questions, they share their selections with a partner. The MLP facilitators encourage the teacher leaders to talk about the affordances and constraints of their selected clips and to anticipate different paths the conversation might take in their workshops. Next, one teacher leader, Candace, volunteers to conduct a rehearsal—showing her selected clip and using her guiding questions to lead a discussion with the whole group—in order to gain experience facilitating a video-based conversation. The MLP leaders, together with the teacher leaders, provide coaching and support, particularly around Candace's introduction and framing of the clip.

Before Candace begins her rehearsal, Karen acknowledges her willingness to take a risk by practicing her facilitation with the whole group. Karen begins, "Thank you, Candace, for volunteering to rehearse your video-based discussion. This can sometimes be scary to do in front of everyone."

Candace responds, "I'm fine. I'm actually glad I get the chance to do it."

Joanie adds, "It can be hard to get up in front of everyone and try this out, but we all learn so much from having someone practice."

Candace responds again, "It's great for me because in my last workshop I told the teachers everything they were going to see in the video instead of letting them watch and react to the video."

Kaitlyn adds, "I think when you have your framing question, and if it is open-ended enough, you can just say the question and let them watch."

As Karen is preparing the video, Joanie suggests, "Candace, why don't you start now by setting up the clip and asking your framing question?"

Candace begins, "This is a clip that one of my teachers, Mike, selected. I really like this clip because Mike brought in cars and stuff to help his students visualize and act out the problem in small groups. Each group had a car and three Monopoly houses and a piece of cardboard so that they could model it. I just think that was so cool."

Mandy suggests, "Candace, it might be better not to share your opinion about the clip. You know, saying that you like it and why you like it. You don't need to say anything. I know you were just telling us, but I think it is better if you just set it up, like, we are going to start by watching how Mike launches the Fuel Gauge Problem."

Jason adds, "Yeah, I agree. Just keep it simple. But I think you can tell them about how Mike brought in manipulatives so the kids could model the problem. It helps explain what they are going to see."

Candace says, "Okay, so let me try again. So today, we are going to watch a short video clip from Mike's classroom. There's a group of kids who are using the fuel gauge as a double number line. Mike had the kids model the problem, and he brought in all of the pieces—cars, houses, markers, and cardboard—for them to use. In this clip, Mike has come over to listen and see how one group is doing. I want you to try to figure out what each kid knows and what each is struggling with."

Joanie comments, "That was well done, Candace. You might want to tell about the modeling first, then mention that there are four kids using a double line and that the teacher is at their table."

Many of the teacher leaders nod in agreement, and then Karen plays the clip. When it ends, Candace repeats her question, "So what did each kid know, and what was each kid struggling with?"

Kaitlyn answers, "The students worked together well, and they knew how to use the double number line. The boy in the red shirt seemed to lead the group, and he knew that when the tank was half full, they could go 300 miles."

Mandy adds, "I think he knew more than that. He figured out all of the benchmark fractions and the related miles."

Jason notes, "He was struggling with figuring out what one tick mark on the fuel gauge was, though."

Candace asks, "What about the girl in the pink shirt? She was doing something different. Did you notice?"

Karen steps in and says, "Candace, that was a great place to refocus the conversation and move on to another student in the video."

The conversation around this rehearsal continues with the teacher leaders actively engaged in analyzing the video and occasionally providing feedback to Candace about her facilitation moves. The workshop concludes with the MLP facilitators encouraging the teacher leaders to use the previously discussed Checklist for Planning PSC Workshops 2 and 3 (refer to Figure 7.6) as they finalize their agendas for Workshop 3.

INSIGHTS FROM THE MLP VIGNETTES

Readers might have a number of questions about learning to facilitate the PSC after reading these vignettes depicting the experiences of one group of teacher leaders engaged in the MLP model. For example, readers might wonder how typical these teacher leaders are, how varied they are in their ability to facilitate the PSC, and what some takeaway messages are for new facilitators and for MLP leaders. As we discuss further in the next chapter, these teacher leaders are typical in the sense that they were "novices"; that is, they did not enter our research project with any experience facilitating (or even knowledge about) the PSC. In fact, most of them did not have experience facilitating professional development of any sort. By the end of the iPSC project, all of the teacher leaders were conducting their workshops with integrity to the key features of the PSC, although there was a distinct range in the skillfulness with which they implemented the PSC. Based on our experiences in the iPSC project, our view is that with sufficient support and motivation, most mathematics teachers can become PSC facilitators. However, in all cases, they will require time, dedicated MLP leadership, and a community of other PSC facilitators within which they can hone their leadership skills and gain confidence as PSC facilitators.

CHAPTER 8

Research on Facilitating the PSC

For teacher leaders to conduct the PSC effectively, what specific facilitation skills will they need to draw on? Which elements of PSC workshops are easier for novice facilitators to enact effectively, and which are more challenging? What moves do strong facilitators make during their PSC workshops, and to what degree is there variation in their facilitation style? In this chapter, we present findings from analyses we have conducted that address each of these questions.

We begin by examining the PSC workshops conducted by novice facilitators, looking carefully at their efforts to establish a productive community and to support the development of knowledge within their groups of teachers. We then look at individual differences among PSC facilitators, using a more fine-grained analysis to unpack the types of facilitation moves two of our strongest facilitators made when they engaged teachers in video-based conversations, contrasting these more skillful facilitators with their less skillful colleagues and also comparing them to one another. Generally, our results indicate that new facilitators can learn to implement the PSC effectively through participation in the MLP program, even using different pedagogical styles. The results also provide some indications as to why certain facilitators are able to foster rich discussions around video better than others, and we speculate about ways to practice and rehearse leading discussions in MLP meetings that would support facilitators of all ability levels.

THE FACILITATION SKILLS OF NOVICE PSC LEADERS

Facilitation of the PSC, and facilitation of professional development in general, requires a unique set of skills and knowledge. Understanding the ways in which the teacher leaders in our research projects were able to implement the PSC with integrity sheds light on how to support the development of these skills. Using data collected from the iPSC project, we analyzed the extent to which the teacher leaders led workshops with integrity to the key features of the PSC, identifying the features of the PSC that they enacted particularly well and the features that were more problematic for them.

These analyses are based on the teacher leaders' facilitation of PSC workshops during years 2 and 3 of the iPSC project. When we say the teacher leaders led the workshops with "integrity" we mean the degree to which the teacher leaders adhered to the intended goals and design of the PD, not whether they rigidly implemented a prescribed set of activities and procedures. Specifically, maintaining integrity to the key features of the PSC entails the following:

- Using a rich mathematical problem as a shared experience
- Facilitating productive discussions about the mathematical content, student thinking, and instructional practices
- Focusing attention on multiple representations and solution strategies
- Using video from the participating teachers' own classrooms

As noted previously, the novice facilitators who took part in the iPSC project were all full-time mathematics teachers who were selected by their school districts to conduct PSC workshops. These teacher leaders prepared to facilitate the PSC at their schools by participating in the Math Leadership Preparation program offered by our research team, as described in Chapters 6 and 7. Table 8.1 provides some demographic information on the teacher leaders. Note that Jordan, Mandy, and Robert joined the iPSC project in Year 1. The other teacher leaders joined in Year 3.

Table 8.1. Teacher Leader Demographic Information

Teacher Leader Name[1]	When Joined iPSC Project	School Name[1]	Years of Experience[2]	Teacher Leader Is Department Chair
Jordan[3]	Year 1	Pride	10	No
Mandy[3]	Year 1	Pride	1	No
Robert	Year 1	Champion	32	Yes
Candace	Year 3	Woodlawn	13	No
Carla	Year 3	Torrence Road	15	Yes
Kaitlyn	Year 3	Four Reed	19	Yes
Kyla[4]	Year 3	Fire Crest	13	No
Jason[4]	Year 3	Fire Crest	20	Yes

1. All names of teacher leaders and schools are pseudonyms.
2. Years of experience refers to the number of years of teaching experience the individual had at the time he or she first joined our study.
3. Jordan and Mandy taught at the same school, but they led separate PSC workshops with different groups of teachers within their school.
4. Kyla and Jason cofacilitated all of the PSC workshops within their school.

We began our analyses of the teacher leaders' facilitation skills by examining the first and last PSC cycles on which we collected data. The first PSC cycle was facilitated by the three teacher leaders who participated in the entire iPSC study: Jordan, Mandy, and Robert. These teacher leaders used the Lemonade Problem, the mixture problem adapted from Van de Walle and colleagues (2007), as described in Chapter 4. During the last PSC cycle, we collected data from all eight teacher leaders (two of whom cofacilitated the PSC for their school). This cycle involved the Fuel Gauge Problem, the ratio-and-rate problem adapted from Jacob and Fosnot (2008) we described in Chapter 7. Following the PSC model, all of the teacher leaders held three workshops per cycle. Twenty-eight of the 30 workshops were videotaped by members of our research team.

We engaged in a detailed examination of these teacher leaders' videotaped workshops. Our goal was to better understand their adherence to the key PSC characteristics and to determine which characteristics of the PSC model were particularly easy or difficult to enact with integrity over time. We wanted to identify the aspects of facilitation where teacher leaders might need additional support and to detect trends that appeared worthy of further investigation. Interviews with the teacher leaders—conducted at the beginning of their participation in the project and after each PSC cycle— along with fieldnotes from our observations of the workshops served as secondary data sources.

We rated the teacher leaders' workshops using an adapted version of the Professional Development Observation Protocol (Banilower & Shimkus, 2004). The observation protocol was designed by Horizon Research, Inc. to evaluate PD sessions using standards for exemplary practice derived from the NCTM's *Principles and Standards for School Mathematics* (2000). It involves rating the entire PD workshop within several categories, each composed of a set of specific indicators. Trained observers watch the video of a workshop and then rate it on each indicator using a 5-point Likert scale, with possible ratings of 1 (not at all) to 5 (to a great extent). In our adaptations to the Professional Development Observation Protocol, we renamed categories to better fit our work, added indicators to reflect the focus of PSC workshops, and omitted indicators that were not relevant to our project.

The categories that we found to be of most relevance are establishing a positive workshop culture, promoting teachers' specialized content knowledge, and promoting teachers' pedagogical content knowledge. Subsets of indicators for these three categories are listed in Tables 8.2–8.4. Because the sample of teacher leaders was small, we did not run tests of statistical significance to compare the two cycles. However, we can see trends in the data and use them to make inferences about the teacher leaders' facilitation of the PSC.

Establishing a Positive Workshop Culture

In terms of workshop culture, we wanted to know about the nature and extent of the participants' engagement in the PSC meetings (see Table 8.2). Specifically, we considered the degree to which the teacher leaders fostered a climate of respect, positive working relationships, active participation, and a willingness to share ideas. We paid close attention to interactions among the teachers in their workshops to see whether they respectfully shared ideas about the content and their instruction, and the extent to which they took intellectual risks such as bringing up something they did not understand.

Overall, the indicators of workshop culture received very high ratings across teacher leaders and across the two PSC cycles. The teacher leaders seemed to have little difficulty garnering a climate of respect and promoting collaborative, collegial working relationships within their groups. In the last cycle, the workshops cofacilitated by Jason and Kyla received the highest ratings. These two teacher leaders were very aware of the importance of building community and thoughtful about ways to encourage participation from all their teachers. For example, prior to having the teachers work through the Fuel Gauge Problem in small groups, Jason and Kyla asked them to individually consider how they and *their* students would approach the problem as well as the difficulties *their* students might encounter when solving it. Such a strategy is likely to build community by engaging all participants in a relevant and safe manner. Jason and Kyla were pleased with the community they saw developing in their math department over the course of the iPSC project. Jason explained in an interview at the end of the year that the PSC workshops enabled teachers to share their ideas more

Table 8.2. Workshop Culture: Average Ratings[1] for Teacher Leaders' PSC Workshops

	CYCLE AVERAGE	
Indicator	First PSC	Last PSC
1. Climate of respect for experiences, ideas, and contributions	4.50	4.55
2. Collaborative working relationship between teacher leader and participants	4.58	4.33
3. Collegial working relationships among participants	4.13	4.60
4. Active participation encouraged and valued	4.14	4.21
5. Participants demonstrated willingness to share ideas and take intellectual risks	3.94	3.90

1. Based on a 5-point Likert scale from 1 (not at all) to 5 (to a great extent)

actively: "That was probably the most awesome thing that happened. We brought sharing out of people, and then it got better as we went on. There was more openness as we went on."

Ratings of participants' willingness to share ideas and take intellectual risks were somewhat lower than other indicators of workshop culture, perhaps because this aspect of community is more challenging to develop and thus takes more time to establish. Kyla recalled the effort she and Jason put into encouraging all their teachers to participate actively, noting, "In the beginning, we had our group of teachers that tended to speak up and share their ideas. We messed around with the grouping a bit as we went through the year, trying to find out which mix was best for getting everyone to share." Jason added, "We've always been a group that doesn't like to share in a large-group setting. This year, we actually broke down those barriers, and now we're more open about discussing things."

Developing and maintaining a professional learning community in which teachers are comfortable working together to improve their teaching is a central component of the PSC model. Throughout the MLP and in the PSC Facilitator's Guide, we provide concrete suggestions for establishing and maintaining community. It seems likely that ongoing, explicit attention to community contributes to teacher leaders' success in enacting this key PD practice beginning in the first year of their facilitation.

Promoting Teachers' Specialized Content Knowledge

Next, we look at teacher leaders' efforts to promote specialized content knowledge (see Table 8.3). As discussed in Chapter 1, specialized content knowledge refers to mathematical content knowledge that is particularly relevant to teaching. We focused especially on the extent to which the teacher leaders helped their teachers develop the mathematical knowledge needed to teach a lesson using the focal PSC problem. We rated this category only for Workshop 1 within each PSC cycle, where specialized content knowledge is foregrounded.

In general, the workshops were rated highly with respect to how often teachers generated and discussed different ways to solve the PSC tasks. Most teacher leaders viewed Workshop 1 primarily as an opportunity to talk about solution strategies, and they were successful in facilitating discussions that explored a variety of representations and methods that could be used in solving the PSC tasks. For instance, one teacher leader, Kaitlyn, described her understanding of Workshop 1 in the following manner: "During the first workshop, we look at a mathematical situation [that is, the PSC task] that can be solved from many different angles or in different ways. And we discuss how we solved it and how we think kids will approach it. We look at the various possible strategies for solving it and we analyze them. And then we talk about planning a lesson for it."

Table 8.3. Specialized Content Knowledge: Average Ratings[1] for Teacher Leaders' PSC Workshops

	CYCLE AVERAGE	
Indicator	First PSC	Last PSC
1. Teachers generate and analyze ways to solve task	4.67	3.93
2. Teachers analyze reasoning used to arrive at correct/incorrect solutions	3.84	2.86
3. Discussion of various solution strategies	4.34	3.86
4. Discussion of relationships among solution strategies	3.34	2.50
5. Discussion of affordances and constraints of various solution strategies	3.67	2.14
6. Discussion of various mathematical representations	3.42	3.07
7. Discussion of relationships among representations	2.92	2.07
8. Discussion of affordances and constraints of various representations	2.59	2.50

1. Based on a 5-point Likert scale from 1 (not at all) to 5 (to a great extent)

In both the first and last cycles, the workshops were typically rated higher on the three indicators addressing the degree to which teachers generated and discussed multiple representations and solution strategies (indicators 1, 3, and 6), compared with the five indicators that entail analyzing reasoning, discussing relationships, and discussing affordances and constraints (indicators 2, 4, 5, 7, and 8). Making comparisons among examples (of solution strategies or representations) is likely to be a more cognitively complex task than exploring individual examples, and as a result, it may require more focused inquiry and workshop time than facilitators were able to devote.

Also, in contrast to workshop culture (Table 8.2) and pedagogical content knowledge (Table 8.4), average ratings on all indicators of specialized content knowledge were lower for the last PSC cycle as compared with the first PSC cycle. We speculate that these lower ratings may be at least partially due to characteristics of the mathematical tasks that were selected for each cycle. Although both tasks can be solved using multiple representations and multiple solution strategies, the Lemonade Problem (used in the first cycle) lends itself to a wider variety of representations and strategies—both correct and incorrect—than does the Fuel Gauge Problem (used in the last cycle).

Promoting Teachers' Pedagogical Content Knowledge

Finally, we looked at the extent to which teacher leaders used strategies designed to deepen teachers' pedagogical content knowledge (see Table 8.4). As you may recall from Chapter 1, these strategies include, for example, engaging teachers in interpreting students' mathematical ideas and purposefully analyzing instructional practices. Given the PSC model's emphasis on using video to situate the discussions in teachers' classrooms, we paid particular attention to the teacher leaders' skills in selecting video clips and framing the discussion of these clips during the workshops. We rated this category only for Workshops 2 and 3 within each PSC cycle, where increasing participants' pedagogical content knowledge is foregrounded.

The teacher leaders were generally successful in choosing clips from the videotaped PSC lessons that were relevant to their teachers and appropriate with respect to the development of community within their groups. They were somewhat less successful, however, in facilitating discussions to deeply analyze instructional practices or student thinking. During our Leader Support Meetings, we focused heavily on the importance of selecting video and formulating questions to launch meaningful discussions, and the data may reflect the teacher leaders' extensive efforts to find appropriate video clips (both during the Leader Support Meetings and on their own time). Navigating video-based discussions during real time in PD workshops is likely to be a more challenging skill than either selecting video clips or

Table 8.4. Pedagogical Content Knowledge: Average Ratings[1] for Teacher Leaders' PSC Workshops

Indicator	CYCLE AVERAGE	
	First PSC	Last PSC
1. Video clips are accessible and relevant to the teachers	4.17	4.29
2. Video clips are appropriate with respect to the level of trust within the community	4.00	4.36
3. Questions about video clips encourage teachers to think deeply about students' mathematical ideas and reasoning	3.67	3.11
4. Teacher leader frames discussions and uses prompts in ways designed to foster development of knowledge of content and students	3.67	3.42
5. Teachers engage in careful unpacking and deep analysis of students' mathematical ideas and reasoning	3.50	3.33
6. Questions about video clips encourage teachers to think deeply about instructional practices	3.00	3.39
7. Teacher leader frames discussions and uses prompts in ways designed to foster development of knowledge of content and teaching	2.88	3.39
8. Teachers engage in careful unpacking and deep analysis of instructional practices	2.88	3.11

1. Based on a 5-point Likert scale from 1 (not at all) to 5 (to a great extent)

developing launching questions, and thus may require additional time and structured guidance for teacher leaders to develop.

Many of the teacher leaders recognized that facilitating discussions about mathematics teaching and learning was an area in which they could benefit from further support. For example, in one of her interviews Candace requested, "I need more help asking the right questions [when showing video]. In one workshop, I had some questions up [on the Smart Board] and that brought better discussion, but I am not always sure what questions are the right ones to ask."

In the first PSC cycle, discussions about students' mathematical ideas and reasoning (indicators 4 and 5) were considerably stronger than discussions about instructional practices (indicators 7 and 8). However, these differences largely disappeared for the last cycle. In their initial PSC workshops, the teacher leaders may have been more comfortable pushing teachers to deeply analyze their students' mathematical reasoning than to critique their own instructional practices. We also hypothesize that, over time, conversations about instruction and student reasoning became more intertwined as the participants became increasingly willing to engage in both of these topics and recognized the degree to which they are connected.

General Patterns in Teacher Leaders' Facilitation of the PSC

It is important to note that our research team on the iPSC project worked with a small number of teacher leaders for an extended period of time to help them learn to facilitate the Problem-Solving Cycle. Also, the group of teacher leaders with whom we worked changed over the course of the project. The findings presented here should be considered tentative, and not necessarily replicable or applicable to all PD contexts. At the same time, these analyses offer a number of insights regarding how novice leaders are likely to facilitate PSC workshops.

In general, the teacher leaders conducted their workshops with integrity to the core principles of the PSC model, thus providing initial evidence that both the PSC and MLP are workable models for districts to implement successfully, and furthermore that the models are both sustainable and scalable. The teacher leaders were particularly successful in creating a climate of respect and trust in their workshops, and establishing collaborative working relationships among the teachers. They also were generally able to engage their groups in discussions of PSC problems focused on multiple mathematical representations and multiple solution strategies. And they were quite capable of selecting video clips that were appropriate for use as springboards for discussions.

We found that there are aspects of implementing the PSC that are especially challenging, and we encourage MLP leaders to focus heavily on developing these facilitation skills. For instance, the teacher leaders were less successful in leading discussions about the affordances, constraints, and mathematical relationships between different representations and solution strategies. They also struggled with orchestrating video-based conversations that maintained a deep level of analysis related to student reasoning or instructional practices. Navigating these discussions about mathematical tasks and classroom video during real time in PD workshops appears to be a challenging and complex skill, and thus PSC facilitators are likely to require ongoing, structured support in order to improve in these areas.

Our analyses of the ratings of teacher leaders' workshops provide a general picture of the strengths and limitations of their facilitation. However, they do not tell us about the nature of the teacher leaders' facilitation moves or the types of moves that are associated with more and less successful PD activities. Because this type of information is important for designing programs to prepare and support teacher leaders, we decided to conduct more fine-grained analyses to explore the facilitation practices that promote deep, substantive discussions about student thinking and pedagogical practices. In the next section, we present the initial results from those analyses, based again on data from the iPSC project.

VARIABILITY IN TEACHER LEADERS' FACILITATION OF VIDEO-BASED DISCUSSIONS

In the previous section, we presented averages of the teacher leaders' workshop ratings. However, we did see differences in the quality of their workshops, with certain teacher leaders earning higher or lower ratings on many of the indicators relative to their colleagues. These individual differences may be a result of variations in the skills and abilities of the teacher leaders, the nature of their PD groups, the school contexts in which they worked, or some combination of factors. In this section, we offer a more fine-grained analysis of their facilitation, focused on the video-based discussions that occurred during Workshops 2 and 3 of their last PSC cycle (using the Fuel Gauge Problem). We examined all the conversations that occurred when the groups watched and discussed video clips during these 14 workshops (2 workshops conducted by each teacher leader/leadership team). Our goals were to identify individual differences in the cognitive depth of the conversations and to explore the variability among the stronger teacher leaders.

Differences in the Cognitive Depth of Conversations

We wanted to investigate the extent to which each facilitator successfully engaged his or her teachers in deep, substantive video-based discussions about student thinking and instructional practices. We refer to this as an analysis of the "cognitive depth" of the teacher leaders' conversations (Van Es, 2011).

First, we organized each discussion into "conversation units" by recording shifts in the focus of the discussion (e.g., from talking about a student's error to considering the teacher's close of the lesson). We then judged the depth of each conversation unit by looking at whether and how the teachers reasoned about what they observed on the video and the degree to which their comments were grounded in evidence from the video.

We categorized each conversation unit as fitting into one of three levels of cognitive depth (see Table 8.5). In Level 1 conversation units, the teachers described or evaluated events in the video with little evidence to support their statements. In Level 2 units, the teachers made interpretative or analytic comments about the events in the video based on evidence. In Level 3 units, the teachers connected events in the video to general principles of teaching and learning, or they proposed alternative pedagogical solutions.

Based on the ratings from the Professional Development Observation Protocol (Banilower & Shimkus, 2004) described earlier in this chapter, we determined that the four strongest teacher leaders/leadership teams overall were Mandy, Jason/Kyla, Kaitlyn, and Carla (see Table 8.6). Our analyses of the conversation units showed that these teacher leaders were also the most successful in terms of leading in-depth video-based discussions. For these four teacher leaders/leadership teams, a larger percentage of their conversation units were characterized as Level 3 compared with the other three teacher leaders. More specifically, during the workshops led by Mandy, Jason/Kyla, Kaitlyn, and Carla, in at least 43% of the conversation units the participants either generalized from the video to other classroom situations or proposed alternative pedagogical moves that a teacher might make in similar situations. In contrast, discussions facilitated by Robert, Jordan, and Candace remained primarily at Level 1 and Level 2. These findings provide additional evidence that there is a clear distinction between teachers who were more capable facilitators and those who were relatively less capable, particularly with respect to the ability to engage teachers in deep, substantive conversations about their students' understanding of content and their own instructional practices.

Differences Among the Stronger Teacher Leaders

Looking more closely at the teacher leaders who were identified as relatively more effective, we wondered how similar their facilitation styles were to one another's. Do they use similar strategies and techniques to engage teachers in deep, substantive discussions of learning and teaching? We conducted an even more in-depth study of the four stronger teacher leaders/leadership teams' video-based discussions in order to unpack the types of facilitation moves that are associated with cognitively rich discussions. Our goal was to understand how these facilitators engaged their participants in connecting the events in the video clips to broader principles of teaching

Table 8.5. Cognitive Depth of Conversation Units

Code	Definition	Example Excerpt	Analysis
LEVEL 1: Describe/ Evaluate	Conversations in which teachers described or evaluated events in the video and provided little evidence to support their comments	After watching a video from one of the teachers in the group, Candace, the facilitator, asks, "What do you notice about what Jenny did and didn't do?" One teacher replies, "I noticed that when she was helping them think through something, she would mention something that she had seen on their paper or heard them talking about. And then she finished with a question, which is great." Another teacher adds, "She just let them figure out their mistakes." A third teacher continues, "She didn't tell them anything."	In this excerpt from a conversation about a video clip from Jenny's Fuel Gauge lesson, Candace asks the teachers to describe what they noticed. Several teachers respond, each adding to the description. Some of the teachers also include an evaluation of Jenny's instruction. In each case, the comment includes no analysis or interpretation.
LEVEL 2: Interpret/ Analyze	Conversations in which teachers made interpretative and/or analytic comments about the events in the video	Teachers in Jason and Kyla's group discuss a student, Jenna, who is stuck. Jason begins the conversation: "In this video, what does Jenna understand about the Fuel Gauge Problem and why is she having trouble?" One teacher speculates, "Initially, Jenna's doing the problem in fractions and she is doing a good job up until the point where she needs to add on the last 120 miles." Another teacher adds, "Yes, I agree. Jenna is on the right track by converting things to fractions but she does not know what to do with the 120 miles." Kyla affirms, "Right. Is there anything else anyone notices about Jenna's understanding of the math?" One teacher suggests, "I think if she was able to stop and think about the problem in miles, then she might be able to see that she can estimate to figure out that Frank has about 7/12 of a tank. But she is not thinking in that way."	In this excerpt, Jason has the teachers analyze the video to discern what the student is thinking and why she is stuck. Two teachers provide initial ideas and then Kyla steps in and restates the question. A third teacher offers another interpretation. Although this teacher suggests what Jenna might do to think more carefully about the problem, she does not propose what the teacher could do to help her.

108

| LEVEL 3: Generalize/ Propose Alternatives | Conversations in which teachers either connected events to general principles of teaching and learning or proposed alternative pedagogical solutions | After watching a video clip from Sue's lesson, Kaitlyn (the teacher leader) draws attention to the way Sue encouraged her students to use the fuel gauge representation as they worked through the problem. Kaitlyn compliments Sue, saying, "I really liked how you had them explain their thinking using the double number line [i.e., the fuel gauge representation]. You kept having them go back to the numbers on the number line, asking, 'What is that number? Tell me what that number means in relationship to the amount of gas in the fuel tank.' I liked how you asked and pointed to the number line, 'What does the 300 mean? How much of the tank is that? What does the 220 mean? Tell me what that number is.' Because kids do throw out a bunch of numbers and then later they're like . . ." At this point, Sue jumps in and completes the thought, "They have no idea how they got it. They're not making sense of their calculation and what the numbers mean." A second teacher chimes in: "I think the questions you asked made them concentrate on number sense." Another teacher nods his head in agreement and says, "I think by having them explain using the fuel gauge, you helped them keep track of the ratios and helped them to think relatively. The double number line is really powerful." Kaitlyn agrees and adds, "Representations can really help students make sense of the math and the ways their peers are thinking. This is kind of like when we used ratio tables and the kids really liked them because they were helpful." | This excerpt focuses on a video clip in which Sue asked two students in a small group to explain how they solved the Fuel Gauge Problem to a third student, who had been absent the previous day. As the students were talking, Sue kept jumping in and asking questions about the numbers that the students were using and having them point out the numbers on the double number line. After Kaitlyn describes and interprets what she sees happening in the clip, the conversation moves to the more generalized idea of using representations to support students' understanding of the mathematics. |

Table 8.6. Teacher Leaders' Average Ratings[1] on Observation Protocol and Cognitive Depth of Video-Based Discussions

Teacher Leader	Average Rating of Video-Based Discussions	Overall (Average) Rating	LEVELS OF COGNITIVE DEPTH[2]		
			Level 3	Level 2	Level 1
Mandy	4.42	4.10	55%	32%	9%
Jason/Kyla	4.22	4.38	44%	11%	33%
Kaitlyn	4.04	4.09	43%	24%	19%
Carla	3.58	3.55	48%	30%	19%
Robert	2.62	3.29	11%	26%	43%
Jordan	2.50	3.14	36%	18%	45%
Candace	1.80	3.13	0	50%	50%

1. Based on a 5-point Likert scale from 1 (not at all) to 5 (to a great extent)
2. Percentages do not always add up to zero because some conversation units were coded "other;" for example, when the teachers leaders focused on aspects of the video clips such as classroom management rather than student thinking or instructional practices.

and learning, or in proposing alternative instructional moves. Interestingly, we found that among these four highly rated teacher leaders, two distinct facilitation techniques emerged. Mandy and Jason/Kyla typically used questions and probes to encourage their teachers to make generalizations and propose alternatives. However, Kaitlyn and Carla were just as likely to offer the generalizations and alternatives themselves and then ask their teachers to engage in conversations about the given ideas. In order to depict the contrasting nature of these two facilitation styles, we created vignettes based on Mandy's and Kaitlyn's workshops that illustrate how they led cognitively rich conversations around video.

In the first vignette, Mandy has just shown a video clip in which one student, Jamie, indicates that she is trying to determine what fraction of gas in the fuel tank is required to travel between Stan's and Louisa's farms. First, Jamie incorrectly sets up the problem as 600 divided by 120, rather than 120 divided by 600. Jamie then converts the problem to 60 divided by 12 and correctly performs the division. However, she adds a zero to the quotient and comes up with the answer 50. Mandy encourages her group to consider how Jamie approached the problem.

Mandy begins, "We need to figure out what this student is doing." Mandy places a large sheet of paper in the center of the table. At her suggestion, the teachers attempt to collaboratively re-create Jamie's strategy. As they are working, the teachers discuss how Jamie set up the ratio in the problem and what the numbers in the ratio represent.

After a lengthy discussion of Jamie's first error, the teachers shift their attention to her second error.

Teacher 1 states, "She's doing 600 divided by 120 and converting it to 60 divided by 12. But you don't just magically take away the zeros. You divide them out and they don't come back."

Teacher 2 speculates that Jamie "took the zeros away to make the division easier, thinking, 'I know I took the zeros away so I need to put them back on.'"

Teacher 3 reflects, "I think that's one thing that confuses kids. When you start saying add zeros or take off zeros, rather than saying you are dividing both numbers by 10, the students don't really know when to do what."

Teacher 2 adds, "I agree. Instead of saying 'drop the zeros', you have to say 'divide them both by 10.'"

Mandy remains quiet during this portion of the teachers' conversation, but she appears to be listening carefully and waiting for the right moment to ask the next question. Once Mandy is confident that the group understands Jamie's approach and the misconceptions underlying Jamie's errors, she encourages them to think about the pedagogical implications.

Mandy raises the question, "What is our concern with them just dropping the zeros? How are we going to address that?"

Teacher 2 responds, "I would ask, 'What is 50 divided by 10? How many 10s are there in 50? And what is 500 divided by 100?' to show that you get the same answer. Then I would ask, 'So, what happens to the zero?'"

Teacher 4 proposes another line of questioning related to the reasonableness of Jamie's answer. She suggests posing the question, "Does it make sense that 120 goes into 600 50 times?"

Building on that suggestion, Teacher 1 adds, "Ask the student to count by 50s and see how long it takes to get to 600. It is not going to be 120 times."

Mandy's two related questions, "What is our concern with them just dropping the zeros?" and "How are we going to address that?," frame Jamie's error as a teachable moment and encourage the group to carefully unpack and understand her solution strategy. This exchange illustrates a common pattern in Mandy's facilitation, which involves posing questions that elicit teachers' ideas about how the students are reasoning, and then prompting them to suggest pedagogical moves that address the students' struggles and errors.

The next vignette is drawn from one of Kaitlyn's workshops based on the Fuel Gauge Problem. Kaitlyn shows a clip from Anna's (one of the teachers in the group) Fuel Gauge lesson, in which a small group of four students is working on the problem. Anna comes over to the group and notices that one student, Mia, does not seem to be following the discussion her peers are having, and steps in to help her. After the teachers watch the video clip, Kaitlyn opens the discussion by highlighting Anna's attempt to help Mia.

Kaitlyn asks, "Do you see how Anna guided the girl in the back?"

Anna immediately shares her concern that she did not provide enough guidance because Mia still seemed really lost.

Kaitlyn refocuses the group on the actions that Anna did take to assist Mia by noting, "But here [pointing to the fuel gauge diagram on the whiteboard], you helped her understand how they got 100 miles as the distance from Louisa's farm to the store. Do you guys see what Anna did?"

Several teachers point out that Anna encouraged Mia to think about traveling from home to school and back. In this way, Anna helped Mia understand what "round-trip" means and then recognize that you have to divide the round-trip distance in half to determine how many miles one way would be.

Kaitlyn agrees, "Yes, she gave her a different problem with different numbers, but it's the same idea. She used a different example to explain that you take half of the round-trip distance. When I watched the video of the lesson, I thought, yes, you can take the same mathematical idea but give Mia a different problem to solve. And then you can say, 'Now this is how that idea will apply to this problem.'"

In this interaction, Kaitlyn brings the cognitive depth of the conversation to Level 3 by sharing her own insights about Anna's instructional move with the group. Kaitlyn focuses the teachers' attention on how Anna addressed Mia's confusion about the idea of a round-trip, and then provides her own interpretation as to why this move was effective. Kaitlyn connects Anna's action to the general pedagogical principle of situating a challenging mathematical concept within a different context—in this case, Anna uses a real-life context that is likely to be more familiar to her students. In contrast to Mandy's "hands-off" facilitation style, Kaitlyn is much more vocal in her group's conversations about the video clips. Kaitlyn frequently steps in to offer generalizations and pedagogical suggestions, rather than eliciting them from the other teachers. As our analyses indicate, both styles of facilitation can lead to engaging discussions at a high cognitive level.

CONCLUDING THOUGHTS ON SUPPORTING TEACHER LEADERS TO BE SKILLFUL FACILITATORS OF THE PSC

Our analyses bring us to the highly encouraging conclusion that novice teacher leaders who take part in the MLP model can successfully lead workshops that closely match the broad outlines and intentions of the PSC model. These teacher leaders varied greatly in their teaching background (as shown in Table 8.1), suggesting that effective PSC facilitators do not necessarily need to be highly experienced teachers or the chair of the mathematics department at their school. Participation in the MLP model very likely was critical to their success.

All of the iPSC teacher leaders led PD in effective ways that were aligned with some of the core principles of the PSC. They consistently focused on relevant goals and activities within their workshops, created supportive professional learning communities, and engaged teachers in conversations around mathematical content and classroom video. At the same time, we also noticed important individual differences among the teacher leaders. One especially intriguing finding was the fact that the four most skillful facilitators used two different and contrasting styles of leading video-based conversations. Two facilitators chose to get critical information on the table by asking probing questions, and the other two offered the information themselves. This finding suggests that there is not necessarily one "right way" to lead conversations in PSC workshops. As is the case with skillful teachers, there is room for pedagogical differences among facilitators.

Similar to teacher preparation programs, leadership preparation programs are vital for individuals who are expected to lead professional development. PD leaders must hold a deeper and more sophisticated knowledge of mathematics, student reasoning, and instructional practices than the teachers who attend their workshops, just as teachers must hold a deeper and more sophisticated knowledge than their students. In addition, PD leaders should be knowledgeable about how to work productively with adult learners and about how to construct environments for teachers to collaborate about relevant topics. The more knowledge and skills related to "best practices" for facilitation that PD leaders gain, the more likely they are to promote learning within their groups. Leadership preparation programs, such as our MLP model, provide teacher leaders with the opportunity to develop these types of knowledge and hone their facilitation skills.

CHAPTER 9

Sustaining and Scaling Up the PSC: One School District's Experience

How can a school district assume ownership of the PSC and ensure that it is a model that will take hold and endure over time? In this chapter, we document the experiences of one district that started using the PSC with the support of our iPSC project team, but ultimately took full responsibility for carrying out the model based on its particular vision for mathematics professional development and relying entirely on its own resources. Over a 3-year period, the goals and structure of the PSC model evolved to fit into the district's changing environment and to accommodate a growing number of teachers and schools. We share the district's experiences from the perspective of its secondary mathematics coordinator, Joanie, and we offer these experiences as an example of the ways the PSC can be adapted in order to be successfully enacted. Throughout the chapter, we include excerpts from audiotaped interviews with Joanie to portray the nature of this process in her own words.

ESTABLISHING THE PSC IN THE CHERRY CREEK DISTRICT

Our research team partnered with the Cherry Creek School District in Centennial, Colorado, in the fall of 2007 to begin using the PSC with the district's middle schools. Cherry Creek is a large, urban school district with approximately 50,000 students enrolled. District leaders envisioned the PSC as a way to address at least three pressing needs: instituting teacher-led mathematics PD in all middle schools, encouraging communication across schools, and promoting instructional leadership. They were hopeful that the PSC would motivate teachers to work collaboratively and view their professional learning time as worthwhile, which would translate into improved classroom practice and increased student achievement.

The basis of our university–school district partnership was that researchers at the university would provide initial preparation and ongoing support to designated teacher leaders, who in turn would implement the PSC at the school level. The researchers worked closely with district leaders to determine the initial parameters of the PD. There was a strong commitment on both sides to maintain frequent and open communication. Over a 3-year time period, the researchers' support for the PSC gradually decreased, and the school district provided gradually increasing support. Finally, in the fourth year, the district took full responsibility for carrying out the PD on a long-term basis using its own resources.

Because Cherry Creek is a historically site-based district, the district administrators did not feel it was appropriate to require either schools or individual teachers to take part in the iPSC project. The administrators agreed to appeal to principals, department chairs, and other appropriate personnel, but all participation was ultimately voluntary and was left up to the discretion of individual school sites. During the first 2 years of our project, 4 of the district's 11 middle schools opted to participate in the program. (Note: The total number of middle schools does not include one charter middle school and one alternative middle school in the district.) Each participating school nominated one or two "teacher leaders" (full-time mathematics teachers) to learn to be PSC facilitators. In Year 1, these teacher leaders met regularly with our research team and the district mathematics coordinator for one semester and then attended a week-long Summer Academy to learn the nuts and bolts of the model. Then, in Year 2, the teacher leaders from three of the four schools agreed to implement the PSC. Although the project started off rather slowly, it steadily gained momentum. In Year 3, six schools elected to participate. By the fourth year, all 11 schools had signed up.

In the first 2 years, members of the research team and the district mathematics coordinator jointly facilitated meetings for the teacher leaders, based on the Mathematics Leadership Preparation model described in Chapter 6. However, during the third year, the mathematics coordinator accepted a position at the state department of education, and the district hired a new mathematics coordinator (formerly a mathematics teacher in one of the district's high schools). The new coordinator, Joanie, worked closely with the research team to plan and facilitate ongoing meetings with teacher leaders. She quickly assumed primary responsibility for managing and overseeing the PSC. As planned, during the fourth year the research team intentionally took a back seat, providing only minimal assistance as Joanie organized and facilitated the Summer Leadership Academy and the Leader Support Meetings that were held during the academic year.

Joanie enthusiastically embraced her new role, and although participation in the PSC was still not required of any school, there was so much positive word of mouth that she found it much easier to recruit participants—including schools and teachers who had previously opted out. Throughout this chapter, we provide excerpts from annual interviews the researchers conducted with Joanie beginning in Year 3 of the iPSC project in order to document her perception of how well the PSC was working in the district, what modifications were taking place, and why. Joanie was determined to capitalize on the momentum of the PSC, not only to continue using the PD and MLP structures that were already in place, but also to expand them.

> This year [i.e., Year 4 of the project] principals are saying, "This PSC professional development is a good thing. It's really changed what my teachers are doing." So, the positive feedback is not just coming from the people who have been involved. The participants are still excited about it, but now other people are starting to pay attention, too. They are saying, "Wait. Those guys are having some cool conversations, and teachers are really engaged in a different way." This is even happening at several of our schools where I would have anticipated some resistance. So that has just been incredibly exciting.
>
> I really feel like the instructional leaders get it, and the departments have all bought in, so it's just sort of this well-oiled machine now. And although I think the PSC is great the way it is, what I see now is that it's a great vehicle to move us forward. The teachers have bought into doing math with one another and having conversations about how kids think. They've bought into looking at one another's videos. I want to take that and capitalize on it, using it to help them grow past where they are right now.

SCALING UP BY EXPANDING AND DISTRIBUTING LEADERSHIP ROLES

In the fourth year of using the PSC, Joanie was awarded a modest amount of money from the district to put her plans in place for organizing an expanded version of the MLP. Specifically, Joanie's plan was to work intensively with a rotating group of middle school mathematics teachers from across the district who would take on a strong leadership role focused on improving mathematics instruction, which would include leading and supporting the implementation of the PSC, creating or revising mathematical tasks, and creating districtwide common assessments. Whereas our research team worked only with teacher leaders who were specifically charged with implementing the PSC in their schools, Joanie's new group of teacher leaders was larger in size and armed with a considerably broader mission. Joanie explained:

> I'm calling them the middle school instructional leadership cadre. It includes the PSC teacher leaders as well as the department coordinators. I have representation from every middle school, with about two to four teachers from each school. The group is a way for me to get information out to the schools. I see these leaders as my conduits to the individual

teachers that I work with. And our work doing the PSC has now been melded into this group.

I meet with the cadre once a month in the afternoon for 3 hours, and twice a year for a full day, which coincides with our district inservice workdays. I want this group to prepare and deliver professional development to the teachers at their schools. That's the agreement that I made with the middle school principals about what this group would do. So, my focus with the group members is on maintaining the Problem-Solving Cycle and maintaining that structure for PD within their schools.

I want to continue that structure and even expand it, creating even more teacher leaders. I want to have even more people with a broader knowledge base around what good instruction looks like, around the standards, around teaching to the standards, around getting kids engaged, and all those pedagogical components. I figure that the more people in a department who have good information, the more quickly those positive changes can happen.

About the same time that Joanie established her middle school leadership cadre, the Common Core State Standards were adopted by the state of Colorado. During her cadre meetings, Joanie encouraged the teacher leaders to consider how they could connect relevant content and practice standards to their PSC workshops. Connecting designated PSC problems to content standards is generally a straightforward process, particularly because Joanie began to select PSC problems from sources that highlight their alignment with the standards. Joanie focused more of her efforts on ensuring that the teacher leaders made explicit connections to the practice standards as they planned, led, and debriefed their PSC workshops.

My focus is on building understanding and a comfort level with the Common Core State Standards for Math Practices. The practice standards perfectly align with the PSC because that sort of thinking is exactly what we want kids to do with the PSC problems. So there's a really nice bridge there. There's been this feeling among the teachers that there's always one more thing they are being asked to do. But now I think they are starting to see that the practice standards are the big thing that we're paying attention to, and we are developing our knowledge and experience with those standards through the Problem-Solving Cycle. I want them to see that the standards and the PSC are not discrete, separate things; they're intertwined and they support each other.

For example, when we're looking at the PSC problems through the lens of the practice standards, we're able to have some common conversations across all grade levels. We can talk about "How did your students use modeling with the problem they were doing?" We can have that conversation with everybody. Even if the 6th-, 7th-, and 8th-graders all did different versions of the problems, they still all used modeling. So we talk about "Well, here was the problem I used, and this is how my kids modeled it." It's an opportunity to have a broad conversation about student thinking.

Another important function of the leadership cadre is to develop and establish multiple teacher leaders within each school. In other words, Joanie's aim is to distribute leadership across a larger number of teachers, thereby promoting a sense of inclusion and capacity-building. To this end, Joanie invites at least one returning teacher leader and one new teacher leader from each school to join her cadre each year. Joanie's long-term goal is to work intensively with a large, diverse, and (to some degree) changing pool of mathematics teachers as part of the cadre. She sees these elements as being key to the success of her overall vision for dramatically improved mathematics instruction and increased student achievement.

Working with the leadership cadre isn't just about me providing professional learning for that small group of people. This is about building capacity. This is about me doing something with the teacher leaders that they take back and do with their own teachers.

Teachers sometimes look at their department chair or the PSC facilitator and ask, "Why do they get to be the leader? Why was that person chosen? Why can't I be a leader?" I see the cadre as being a more fluid group, where teachers participate for a school year. And then maybe the next school year there's one or two people who are changed out from each school. It really gives everyone the opportunity to get intensive PD from the district level. And it's an opportunity to talk within a group of teachers from different schools. It doesn't become exclusive; it becomes expansive.

This approach is about more people carrying the same message, so that when they go back to their schools they're not the only people who have heard the message. And they're not the only person who is trying to make changes in their department. There is still a point person at each middle school for the PSC, but more people in their department will have heard the same message from the district level.

It's just getting more people in the room to have that deeper level of thinking about what they are doing, rather than having the PSC facilitator being the only person who has all this knowledge and being the one who has to impart the information. That's a lot to ask of one person.

WHAT ACCOUNTS FOR THE SUCCESS OF THE PSC IN CHERRY CREEK?

We have several theories about what led to the adoption and sustainable implementation of the PSC model by the schools and teachers throughout the Cherry Creek district, including those who initially elected not to participate. First, the nature and design of the PSC ensured that there was a comfortable balance of structure and flexibility. Joanie implemented key structural elements of the PSC, such as teachers working collaboratively to solve a rich, open-ended mathematical problem; teaching the problem; and discussing video clips from their PSC lessons. At the same time, she took advantage of the flexibility that was intentionally built into the PSC to do the following:

- Encourage teachers to modify the selected problem and construct individual lesson plans to reflect their students' needs
- Support facilitators to identify learning goals for their groups that influenced their selection and viewing of video
- Organize meetings for teacher leaders in a manner that allowed a wide variety of teachers to assume leadership positions

This flexibility is especially critical at a district like Cherry Creek in which schools operate under a good deal of local control and autonomy. Feeling comfortable adapting specific elements of the PSC empowered Joanie and the teacher leaders to make modifications as they deemed necessary and appropriate.

Second, the PSC took hold in Cherry Creek by enabling the district to build its internal leadership capacity, which remains a central district goal. Whereas many PD models require an outside specialist or perhaps a coach with little or no classroom teaching responsibilities to take on the facilitation role, the PSC can be facilitated by a regular, full-time mathematics teacher. However, just as teachers rely on facilitators to organize and lead structured professional learning opportunities, facilitators rely on district administrators to provide ongoing leadership training and support. Joanie put into place a mechanism for teacher leaders to develop their facilitation skills, enabling them to meet and plan together on a regular basis, share their experiences across schools and grades, and learn from one another as both teachers and PD leaders. Joanie took her role as point person seriously and frequently checked in with the facilitators even outside of their regular cadre meetings. When necessary, she corresponded with individual teachers who had concerns related to the PD and she attended PSC workshops at several schools. Joanie's vision for a large and skilled "leadership cadre," coupled with administrative backing and resources, has served to maintain the momentum that was built during the first few years and has propelled the PSC forward in Cherry Creek for the foreseeable future.

I really feel like one of the most powerful pieces has been that somebody doesn't just come into the school to do this, but we're building on the expertise of people already there. And I think that's part of what has made the PSC sustainable in the district. It's not like there is some magic thing coming in from the outside that's giving some great information about becoming better teachers. The teacher leaders are creating it, and that allows them to make it really specific to their teachers' needs, their department's needs, and their students' needs.

In the past, when we worked at the district level around the PSC, it was just with the teacher leaders who facilitated it. Now I've got this expanded group of leaders and everyone in the room has experienced the PSC in some form (as teachers or as facilitators). It's just amazing how the common language and the common experiences have created this different environment in the cadre meetings. The participants all know they're talking about the same thing. It's like, "Yes, we did that, too." So there's a lot of power in that. It's definitely something the teacher leaders are really continuing to be excited about. It's become a cultural norm.

BEGINNING TO WORK WITH HIGH SCHOOL TEACHER LEADERS

Although the iPSC project initially focused exclusively on middle schools, during Year 5, Joanie established a cadre of high school mathematics teacher leaders. She included three teachers from each high school in this new group: one teacher from each of three courses—Algebra 1, Algebra 2, and Geometry. Like the members of the middle school mathematics leadership cadre, the high school teacher leaders met monthly and worked together on a number of district priorities, including preparing themselves to lead the PSC in their schools.

At first, Joanie encountered a good deal of resistance from the high school cadre, and she had to focus heavily on guiding them to recognize the importance of professional development based on investigations of student thinking and classroom instruction. She led the group through a modified version of the PSC, in their role as classroom teachers, similar to how our research team initially worked with the middle school teacher leaders. However, she modified the PSC in two important ways for the high school teachers. First, each of the three groups of teachers (Algebra 1, Algebra 2, and Geometry) selected and used different PSC problems. Second, Joanie did not prompt the teachers to videotape their lessons. Instead, she encouraged them to collect and then analyze their students' work on the selected problem. The intention behind these modifications was to make the PSC more appealing to the high school teachers, to garner a stronger buy-in during the beginning stages of their work together, and to lessen the logistical burdens associated with videotaping.

> I put them in three groups [Algebra 1, Algebra 2, and Geometry] and gave each group four or five problems. I said that the first step is to choose a focus and agree on a problem that you're all going to do. And then they went through the Problem-Solving Cycle work of scoping it out, identifying the mathematics, thinking about how students would engage with the problem, and thinking about places students might stumble or get off-track.
>
> I took them through that whole process. And then I said, "Okay, the expectation is that each of you in the cadre will go back and teach this problem in your own classroom." I knew I didn't have the logistical support for them to do video, so I replaced the video part with having them gather student work. I told them, "I expect you will have taught this problem and will come back to debrief us on how it went. And then bring in representative student work. Don't just bring all your top students' work. It's not about showing off. This is about becoming a better teacher and supporting one another in doing that."
>
> So that's what we did. The month they came back after having taught the problem, they were just so excited. The whole group—it was like a light bulb went on. And they were like, "I get what you want us to do. I get why you formed this cadre. I get why there's power in this."

Joanie felt satisfied that she had met her goal of establishing a positive culture and ensuring that the high school cadre would commit to continued professional development using the PSC. She was also encouraged that she could work with a highly diverse group of teachers and help them find common ground. Especially by integrating the structure of the PSC with an emphasis on exploring the Common Core's practice standards, Joanie helped these teachers see the value in their cadre meetings. Encouraged by this experience with what she called her "most resistant teachers," Joanie anticipated pushing forward with a more formalized plan for using the PSC with the high school cadre, and ultimately persuading them to take this form of PD back to their school-based professional learning communities.

> I see this year as a transition. I really think that next school year there is going to be more opportunities for the structure of the PSC to be formalized. I think it is the time now. I think things are in place enough. I really had to create a sense of urgency and get folks focused on the new Common Core standards. And now we'll work on developing the leadership and facilitation skills of those people who are going to be

leading professional learning communities. It's just a matter of getting everybody to see that urgency. I think we're right on the brink of it.

A BRIGHT FUTURE FOR THE PSC IN CHERRY CREEK

The PSC has benefited from consistent positive feedback from teachers, teachers leaders, and administrators throughout the Cherry Creek School District. Over time, sustaining and even scaling up the PSC has grown easier thanks to increased principal support and an ongoing mechanism for teacher leaders across the district to regularly meet together. Of course, the strong vision, commitment, and leadership skills of the district's secondary mathematics coordinators has been the force that brought all the necessary pieces together and is the glue that continues to hold them in place.

As Kennedy, Deuel, Nelson, and Slavit (2011) argue, "By acknowledging and using teachers' knowledge and expertise, and by giving teachers different forms of leadership positions and control of their learning groups, their knowledge and expertise will grow and deepen. Teachers will begin to take the wheel and drive their own learning" (p. 24). Certainly in Cherry Creek, a combination of the structure of the PSC, an emphasis on promoting and distributing leadership, and a commitment to the long-term goals of improving mathematics teaching and learning has led to positive outcomes and has fostered the district's determination to continue along this path. Because the district has now established an internal structure for the PSC facilitators to be supported on a regular basis, the PD has, in effect, become a districtwide initiative for Cherry Creek's secondary mathematics teachers.

Epilogue

In this book we describe our journey thus far into the development, implementation, and research on the Problem-Solving Cycle and the Mathematics Leadership Preparation models. Over the past decade, we have spent many hours in teachers' classrooms, professional development workshops, and leadership preparation meetings—sometimes as instructional leaders or PD providers, but always as reflective observers. Based on these experiences, and the in-depth analyses of our research data, the most important message we have to share is the importance of ongoing and relevant professional learning opportunities for teachers. In particular, we would argue that these opportunities should have as their foundation a supportive and collaborative environment, in which teachers' classrooms and voices are the primary components and the focus is on unpacking the complexity of classroom teaching and student learning.

Schools and districts are seeking ways to strengthen mathematics teaching in order to improve student learning. There is some urgency in this charge, and we believe the power of the PSC lies in bringing mathematics teachers together on a continual basis to identify goals that are currently important and to hone their craft. An in-house model, the PSC is an alternative to (and can complement) one-on-one coaching models or PD efforts that require outside experts and extensive resources.

In mathematics, as in other subject areas, knowledgeable and skilled teachers are essential to ensure student success. More than ever, high expectations around classroom teaching and student achievement—coupled with increasing pressures of accountability—have resulted in a growing demand for professional learning opportunities for teachers that are effective, scalable, and sustainable. At the same time, because of wide variations in local contexts and needs, professional development cannot be construed as a "one-size-fits-all" matter. Therefore, while the Problem-Solving Cycle and the accompanying Mathematics Leadership Preparation models offer a vision and a structure for school-based professional learning, they are also intentionally designed to be flexible and adaptable.

The PSC can readily be tailored to meet a district or school's priorities in the areas of mathematical content, student thinking, and instructional practices. Given the nature of current educational reform efforts, it is especially critical for teachers to attend to, understand, and build on their students' thinking. The PSC offers a new way for teachers to become increasingly capable in this regard. Furthermore, the nature of PSC workshops ensures that teachers will engage in activities that are personally relevant, drawing from their own expertise and that of their colleagues. As was the case in the Cherry Creek School District (discussed in Chapter 9), restructuring existing professional development or professional learning community time into PSC workshops—while maintaining a focus on effectively implementing state standards and district priorities—can lead to a smooth transition to a new model of PD.

Just as the PSC provides ongoing professional learning for teachers, the MLP provides the same continuous learning for leaders of the PSC. Fostering the development of teacher leaders is essential to building local capacity to provide long-term professional development for all teachers. It is also an important way to distribute leadership among teachers in a school or district. Yet there are few existing and even fewer researched models that prepare teachers to facilitate high-quality PD. The MLP enables schools and districts to capitalize on their own human resources and support teachers with a range of classroom experiences and pedagogical approaches to lead structured, site-based PSC workshops. By incorporating the PSC along with the MLP, mathematics departments can take professional learning into their own hands and ensure that it addresses the immediate needs of their schools, their teachers, and their students.

Further Readings on the PSC

Borko, H. (2012). Designing scalable and sustainable professional development: The Problem-Solving Cycle and teacher leader preparation. In M. Glaser-Zikuda, T. Seidel, C. Rohlfs, A. Groschner, & S. Ziegelbauer (Eds.), *Mixed methods in empirical educational research* (pp. 259–271). Munster, Germany: Waxmann.

Borko, H., Frykholm, J., Pittman, M., Eiteljorg, E., Nelson, M., Jacobs, J., Koellner-Clark, K., & Schneider, C. (2005). Preparing teachers to foster algebraic thinking. *Zentralblatt für Didaktik der Mathematik: International Reviews on Mathematical Education, 37*(1), 43–52.

Borko, H., Jacobs, J., Eiteljorg, E., & Pittman, M. E. (2008). Video as a tool for fostering productive discourse in mathematics professional development. *Teaching and Teacher Education, 24,* 417–436.

Borko, H., Jacobs, J., & Koellner, K. (2010). Contemporary approaches to teacher professional development. P. Peterson, E. Baker, & B. McGaw (Eds.), *International Encyclopedia of Education, Vol. 7* (pp. 548–556). Oxford, England: Elsevier.

Borko, H., Jacobs, J., Seago, N., & Mangram, C. (2014). Facilitating video-based professional development: Planning and orchestrating productive discussions. In Y. Li, E. A. Silver, & S. Li (Eds.), *Transforming mathematics instruction: Multiple approaches and practices* (pp. 259–281). Cham, Switzerland: Springer International.

Borko, H., & Klingner, J. (2014). Supporting teachers in schools to improve their instructional practice. In B. J. Fishman, W. R. Penuel, A. R. Allen, & B. H. Cheng (Eds.), *Design-based implementation research: Theories, methods, and exemplars* (*National Society for the Study of Education Yearbook, 112*(2), pp. 274–297). New York, NY: Teachers College, Columbia University.

Borko, H., Koellner, K., & Jacobs, J. (2011, March 4). Meeting the challenges of scale: The importance of preparing professional development leaders. *Teachers College Record.* www.tcrecord.org (ID Number: 16358)

Borko, H., Koellner, K., & Jacobs, J. (2014). Examining novice teacher leaders' facilitation of mathematics professional development. *Journal of Mathematical Behavior, 33,* 149–167.

Borko, H., Koellner, K., Jacobs, J., & Seago, N. (2011). Using video representations of teaching in practice-based professional development programs.
*Zentralblatt für Didaktik der Mathematik: International Reviews on Math-
ematical Education, 43*(1), 175–187.

Borko, H., Virmani, R., Khachatryan, E., & Mangram, C. (2014). The role of
video-based discussions in professional development and the preparation of
professional development leaders. In B. D. Calandra & P. Rich (Eds.), *Digital
video for teacher education: Research and practice* (pp. 89–108). Philadel-
phia, PA: Routledge.

Clark, K. K., Jacobs, J., Pittman, M., & Borko, H. (2005). Strategies for building
mathematical communication in the middle school classroom: Modeled in
professional development, implemented in the classroom. *Current Issues in
Middle Level Education, 11(2),* 1–12.

Jacobs, J., Borko, H., & Koellner, K. (2009). The power of video as a tool for
professional development and research: Examples from the Problem-Solving
Cycle. In T. Janik & T. Seidel (Eds.), *The power of video studies in investigating teaching and learning in the classroom* (pp. 259–273). Munster, Germany:
Waxmann.

Jacobs, J., Borko, H., Koellner, K., Schneider, C., Eiteljorg, E., & Roberts, S. A.
(2007). The Problem-Solving Cycle: A model of mathematics professional
development. *Journal of Mathematics Education Leadership, 10(1),* 42–57.

Jacobs, J., Koellner, K., & Funderburk, J. (2012). Problem solved: Middle school
math instruction gets a boost from a flexible model for learning. *Journal of
Staff Development, 33*(2), 32–39.

Jacobs, J., Koellner, K., John, T., & King, C. (2014). The process of instructional
change: Insights from the Problem-Solving Cycle. In Y. Li, E. A. Silver, & S.
Li (Eds.), *Transforming mathematics instruction: Multiple approaches and
practices* (pp. 335–354). Cham, Switzerland: Springer International.

Koellner, K., & Jacobs, J. (2015). Distinguishing models of professional development: The case of an adaptive model's impact on mathematics teachers'
knowledge, instruction, and student achievement. *Journal of Teacher Education, 66*(1), 51–67.

Koellner, K., Jacobs, J., & Borko, H. (2011). Mathematics professional development: Critical features for developing leadership skills and building teachers' capacity. *Mathematics Teacher Education and Development, 13*(1),
115–136.

Koellner, K., Jacobs, J., Borko, H., Roberts, S., & Schneider, C. (2011). Professional development to support students' algebraic reasoning: An example
from the Problem-Solving Cycle Model. In J. Cai & E. Knuth (Eds.), *Early
algebraization: A global dialogue from multiple perspectives* (pp. 429–452).
New York, NY: Springer.

Koellner, K., Jacobs, J., Borko, H., Schneider, C., Pittman, M., Eiteljorg, E., Bunning, K., & Frykholm, J. (2007). The Problem-Solving Cycle: A model to

support the development of teachers' professional knowledge. *Mathematical Thinking and Learning, 9(3)*, 271–303.

Koellner, K., Schneider, C., Roberts, S., Jacobs, J., & Borko, H. (2008). Using the Problem-Solving Cycle model of professional development to support novice mathematics instructional leaders. In F. Arbaugh & P. M. Taylor (Eds.), *Inquiry into mathematics teacher education* (pp. 59–70). San Diego, CA: Association of Mathematics Teacher Educators.

References

Ball, D. L., Hill, H. C., & Bass, H. (2005). Knowing mathematics for teaching: Who knows mathematics well enough to teach third grade, and how can we decide? *American Educator, Fall*, 14–46.

Ball, D. L., Thames, M. H., & Phelps, G. (2008). Content knowledge for teaching: What makes it special? *Journal of Teacher Education, 59*, 389–407.

Banilower, E. R., & Shimkus, E. S. (2004). *Professional development observation study*. Chapel Hill, NC: Horizon Research. Retrieved from www.pdmathsci.net/reports/banilower_shimkus_2004.pdf

Desimone, L. M. (2009). Improving impact studies of teachers' professional development: Toward better conceptualizations and measures. *Educational Researcher, 38*(3), 181–199.

Driscoll, M. (1999). *Fostering algebraic thinking: A guide for teachers, grades 6–10*. Portsmouth, NH: Heinemann.

Driscoll, M., DiMatteo, R. W., Nikula, J., Egan, M., Mark, J., & Kelemanik, G. (2008). *The fostering geometric thinking toolkit: A guide for staff development*. Portsmouth, NH: Heinemann.

Hill, H. C., Sleep, L., Lewis, J. M., & Ball, D. L. (2007). Assessing teachers' mathematical knowledge: What knowledge matters and what evidence counts? In F. K. Lester Jr. (Ed.), *Second handbook of research on mathematics teaching and learning* (pp. 111–155). Charlotte, NC: Information Age Publishing.

Jacob, B., & Fosnot, C. T. (2008). *Best buys, ratios, and rates*. Portsmouth, NH: Heinemann.

Kennedy, A., Deuel, A., Nelson, T. H., & Slavit, D. (2011). Requiring collaboration or distributing leadership? *Phi Delta Kappan, 92*(8), 20–24.

Kilday, C. R., & Kinzie, M. B. (2009). An analysis of instruments that measure the quality of mathematics teaching in early childhood. *Early Childhood Education Journal, 36*, 365–372.

Learning Forward. (2011). *Standards for professional learning*. Oxford, OH: Author. Retrieved from www.learningforward.org/standards/standards.cfm

Learning Mathematics for Teaching Project. (2011). Measuring the mathematical quality of instruction. *Journal of Mathematics Teacher Education, 14*, 25–47.

LeFevre, D. M. (2004). Designing for teacher learning: Videobased curriculum design. In J. Brophy (Ed.), *Advances in research on teaching: Vol. 10. Using video in teacher education* (pp. 235–258). Oxford, England: Elsevier.

Loucks-Horsley, S., Stiles, K. E., Mundry, S. E., Love, N., & Hewson, P. W. (2009). *Designing professional development for teachers of science and mathematics.* Thousand Oaks, CA: Corwin Press.

National Council of Teachers of Mathematics (NCTM). (2000). *Principles and standards for school mathematics.* Reston, VA: Author.

National Council of Teachers of Mathematics (NCTM). (2014). *Principles to actions: Ensuring mathematical success for all.* Reston, VA: Author.

National Governors Association Center for Best Practices & Council of Chief State School Officers. (2010). *Common Core State Standards for Mathematics.* Washington, DC: Author.

Schrock, C., Norris, K., Pugalee, D. D., Seitz, R., & Hollingshead, F. (2013). *Great tasks for Mathematics K–5.* Reston, VA: NCTM.

Schrock, C., Norris, K., Pugalee, D. D., Seitz, R., & Hollingshead, F. (2013). *Great tasks for Mathematics 6–12.* Reston, VA: NCTM.

Schwartz, J. L., & Kenney, J. M. (1995). *The "-ness" tasks.* Cambridge, MA: Balanced Assessment Program, Harvard Graduate School of Education.

Seidel, T., Stürmer, K., Blomberg, G., Kobarg, M., & Schwindt, K. (2011). Teacher learning from analysis of videotaped classroom situations. Does it make a difference whether teachers observe their own teaching or that of others? *Teaching and Teacher Education, 27,* 259–267.

Shulman, L. S. (1986). Those who understand: Knowledge growth in teaching. *Educational Researcher, 15*(2), 4–14.

Van de Walle, J. A., Karp, K. S., & Bay-Williams, J. M. (2007). *Elementary and middle school mathematics: Teaching developmentally.* Boston, MA: Pearson.

Van Es, E. A. (2011). A framework for learning to notice student thinking. In M. G. Sherin, V. R Jacobs, & R. A. Philipp (Eds.), *Mathematics teacher noticing: Seeing through teachers' eyes* (pp. 134–151). New York, NY: Routledge.

Zhang, M., Lundeberg, M. A., Koehler, M. J., & Eberhardt, J. (2011). Understanding affordances and challenges of three types of video for teacher professional development. *Teaching and Teacher Education, 27,* 454–462.

Index

About the Authors

Hilda Borko is a professor of education at Stanford University. She received her BA in psychology, MA in philosophy of education, and PhD in educational psychology from the University of California, Los Angeles. Dr. Borko was a middle and high school teacher for 4 years. Her research explores teacher cognition, the process of learning to teach, and the impact of teacher professional development programs on teachers and students. Dr. Borko served as president of the American Educational Research Association (2003–2004). She is a member of the National Academy of Education and the 2014 recipient of the Excellence in Scholarship in Mathematics Teacher Education Award from the Association of Mathematics Teacher Educators.

Jennifer Jacobs is a research faculty associate in the Institute of Cognitive Science at the University of Colorado Boulder. She received her BA in psychology and Japanese from the University of Michigan, and her MA and PhD in psychology from the University of California, Los Angeles. Dr. Jacobs's research focuses on classroom teaching practices, teachers' attitudes and beliefs, and programs of professional development to support teacher and student learning.

Karen Koellner is a professor of mathematics education at Hunter College, City University of New York. She received her BS in liberal studies from the University of Southern California, her MA in curriculum and instruction from California State University, Los Angeles, and her PhD in mathematics education from Arizona State University. Dr. Koellner was a middle school mathematics teacher for 8 years and continues to actively work in schools conducting research and professional development with inservice and preservice teachers. Dr. Koellner's research focuses on mathematics teacher professional development, students' mathematical thinking, and field-based experiences for preservice teachers in urban contexts.

Lyn E. Swackhamer is a research associate at RMC Research Corporation in Denver, Colorado. She received her BA in accounting from North Georgia State College and University and her MA in curriculum and instruction and PhD in educational leadership and innovation from the University of

Colorado Denver. Dr. Swackhamer taught at the elementary, middle school, and college level for 8 years and brought that experience to her current work as a researcher and evaluator. At RMC Research, she has led evaluation efforts for clients such as NASA and the Rocky Mountain Middle School MSP and also conducts technical assistance projects for the Regional Education Laboratory for the Central States.